A SHORT HISTORY
OF LITERARY ENGLISH

A SHORT HISTORY
OF LITERARY ENGLISH

Second Edition

W. F. BOLTON
Professor of English, Douglass College of Rutgers University

EDWARD ARNOLD

© W. F. BOLTON 1972

First published 1967 by
Edward Arnold (Publishers) Ltd
25 Hill Street, London W1X 8LL
Second Edition 1972
Reprinted 1974

Cloth edition ISBN 0 7131 5649 X
Paper edition ISBN 0 7131 5650 3

Printed in Great Britain by
Unwin Brothers Limited, Old Woking, Surrey
A member of the Staples Printing Group

Foreword

This book aims to provide a sketch of the history of the English language for those beginning the study of English literature. In such a small compass much has had to be omitted; the principle of selection has been relevance to the literary language.

All language is primarily spoken: the written language is a comparatively recent development (perhaps the last 5000 years; human speech may be on the order of a hundred times as old), and writing comes later than, and is modelled on, speech in the experience of individuals. None the less, the written language has features of its own. Many people, moreover, encounter nearly as much writing as speech, especially when they are students. By 'literary English' I mean broadly the written language as it appears in works of literature, without necessarily suggesting that it is something wholly apart from other written English; that is, I define the language by the literature in which it appears, rather than the literature by the language it employs.

The history of a language can be studied from two points of view: that of the changes in its sounds, spellings, vocabulary, and forms; and that of the opinions about it. The two are often called the 'internal' and the 'external' respectively. The second has particular importance in the literary connexion, but developments in the two rarely go hand-in-hand. For this reason I have devoted separate parts of the book to them. (Texts in Part II are normalized; those in Part I are not.)

In addition to this division, the book differs from others in its brevity, its concentration on matters of literary importance, and its exclusion of long lists of items—especially examples of vocabulary—in isolation. Yet fuller treatments elsewhere are valuable and necessary to an understanding of the issues touched on here, and this book does not seek to take their place. The introductory bibliography and the others at the end of each chapter mention some of the places in which further material can be found. I have restricted these lists to books which would be reasonably available, and so I have omitted highly specialized, foreign-language, and all but a few pre-World War II items. The books I have listed will usually contain a guide to the next stage of study and to the older and foreign-language works. All the same, the lists are rather long, not because every item on them is essential at this stage, but because not every item may be obtainable: readers who cannot find one may have better luck with another. (The date given is for the most recent edition or reprinting I know of.)

It remains for me to thank those without whom this book could not have been written. The lists of further reading suggest in some measure my great debt to other workers in the field. My students at the University of Reading have cheerfully undergone exposure to some of the ideas embodied in this book, and told me what they thought of them. Miss J. M. Field has been of indispensable aid at every stage of the book's preparation, from first plan to final proof. And my wife, who read and re-read the manuscript, has made many valuable corrections and suggestions in 'the educated speech of south-east England', to the improvement of my book and the enlightenment of my American viewpoint. Such a short book, of which the failings are my own, is a sparse testimony to the benefits they have all done me.

Foreword to the Second Edition

A second edition has provided the opportunity to correct some errors, and to bring the bibliographies up to date as far as the end of 1971.

Contents

Acknowledgements

The text of *The Authorized Version of the Bible* is Crown copyright, and extracts used herein are reproduced by permission. The extract from *The Bible in Basic English*, 1941, is reproduced by permission of Cambridge University Press and Evans Brothers Ltd; the extract from *The Gospels in Modern English* translated by J. B. Phillips, 1952, by permission of Geoffrey Bles Ltd; the extract from *The New English Bible, New Testament*, 1961, by permission of Oxford and Cambridge University Presses.

For Further Reading

HISTORIES OF THE ENGLISH LANGUAGE:

H. Alexander, *The Story of our Language*, 1962.

C. Barber, *The Flux of Language*, 1965 (also published as *The Story of Language*, 1964).

L. Barnett, *The Treasure of our Tongue*, 1966.

A. C. Baugh, *A History of the English Language*, 1957.

M. Bloomfield and L. Newmark, *A Linguistic Introduction to the History of English*, 1964.

H. Bradley, *The Making of English*, 1957.

G. L. Brook, *A History of the English Language*, 1963.

M. M. Bryant, *Modern English and its Heritage*, 1962.

O. Jespersen, *The Growth and Structure of the English Language*, 1956.

L. M. Myers, *The Roots of Modern English*, 1966.

J. Nist, *A Structural History of English*, 1966.

M. Pei, *The Story of English*, 1953.

R. A. Peters, *A Linguistic History of English*, 1968.

S. Potter, *Our Language*, 1959.

T. Pyles, *The Origins and Development of the English Language*, 1971.

S. Robertson and F. G. Cassidy, *The Development of Modern English*, 1960.

L. P. Smith, *The English Language*, 1966.

R. D. Stevick, *English and its History*, 1968.

B. M. H. Strang, *A History of English*, 1970.

C. L. Wrenn, *The English Language*, 1958.

H. C. Wyld, *The Growth of English*, 1954.

H. C. Wyld, *A History of Modern Colloquial English*, 1936.

H. C. Wyld, *A Short History of English*, 1949.

E. Weekley, *The English Language*, 1952.

F. T. Wood, *An Outline History of the English Language*, 1969.

AMERICAN ENGLISH

C. M. Babcock, *The Ordeal of American English*, 1961.

J. P. Friend, *The Development of American Lexicography, 1798–1864*, 1967.

G. P. Krapp, *The English Language in America*, 1960.

M. M. Mathews, *Beginnings of American English*, 1963.

H. L. Mencken, *The American Language*, 1947 (*Supplements*, 1952, 1948).

T. Pyles, *Words and Ways of American English*, 1952.

C. E. Reed, *Dialects of American English*, 1967.
R. W. Shuy, *Discovering American Dialects*, 1967.

ENGLISH VOCABULARY:

J. B. Greenough and G. L. Kittredge, *Words and their Ways in English Speech*, 1914.
A. S. C. Ross, *Etymology*, 1958.
M. S. Serjeantson, *A History of Foreign Words in English*, 1961.
The Oxford English Dictionary, 1933 (Supplement, 1933).
J. A. Sheard, *The Words we Use*, 1954.

TEXTS ILLUSTRATING THE HISTORY OF THE ENGLISH LANGUAGE:

W. F. Bolton, *The English Language*, 1966.
W. F. Bolton and D. Crystal, *The English Language*, 1969.
C. Davies, *English Pronunciation from the Fifteenth to the Eighteenth Century*, 1934.
A. E. Farnham, *A Sourcebook in the History of English*, 1969.
R. L. Hoffman, *History of the English Language*, 1968.
A. M. Markman and E. R. Steinberg, *English Then and Now*, 1970.
A. G. Rigg, *The English Language*, 1968.
C. T. Scott and J. L. Erickson, *Readings for the History of the English Language*, 1968.
S. I. Tucker, *English Examined*, 1961.

THE ROLE OF LANGUAGE IN ENGLISH LITERATURE:

G. L. Brook, *The Language of Dickens*, 1970.
D. Davie, *Articulate Energy*, 1955.
I. A. Gordon, *The Movement of English Prose*, 1966.
G. Lawton, *John Wesley's English*, 1962.
G. N. Leech, *A Linguistic Guide to English Poetry*, 1969.
J. Miles, *Renaissance, Eighteenth-Century, and Modern Language in English Poetry*, 1960.
W. M. Nowottny, *The Language Poets Use*, 1962.
G. H. Vallins, *The Pattern of English*, 1957.
G. Watson, *Literary English since Shakespeare*, 1970.

(See also the lists at the end of each chapter, especially chapter 8.)

I   *The Internal History*

CHAPTER ONE

Old English

Old English is the name given to the closely related dialects
spoken in England from the fifth century, when raiders from
north Germany began their settlements, until the eleventh
century, when the effects of the Norman Conquest began to
appear in the language. The Germanic settlers came from three
tribes, the Jutes, Angles and Saxons (Old English is often called
Anglo-Saxon); and the Jutes became established in the extreme
south-east of the country, the Saxons in the south-west, and the
Angles in the part north of the Thames. From the period of the
settlement, then, there were regional dialect differences in England
corresponding to the regional differences in north Germany:
Kentish in the area of the Jutes, West Saxon in that of the Saxons,
Anglian in that of the Angles. But little evidence of the language
survives from earlier than the eighth century, half-way through
the six hundred years or so during which Old English was spoken,
and even the earliest evidence reveals dialect differences additional
to those the settlers brought with them, notably in the Anglian
area: here Mercian, spoken between the Thames and the Humber,
differed from Northumbrian, spoken north of the Humber.
Even to the end of the period the evidence for some areas
continues to be so slight that our knowledge, for example, of
Northumbrian is limited to the linguistic forms common to a
few inscriptions, some glosses (interlinear translations of Latin
texts), and three poems; we cannot say what written, much less
spoken, Northumbrian was like beyond that.

For some of the four main dialects of Old English there is better evidence: Kentish is not well represented, but Mercian is, and West Saxon survives in a great number of varied documents, particularly from the later part of the period. The difference results from a number of causes which have nothing to do with the 'quality' of the dialects. In the south-west, the political and cultural centre of the country from the reign of Alfred onward, conditions favoured the use of the vernacular and the preservation of manuscripts. Hence our knowledge of Old English is concentrated on the literary and other remains in West Saxon dating from about 900 onwards, and on the language in which they are written.

This Old English was already a language with a long history which we can trace, although not from written records. Just as we accord a common name to the shared linguistic features which characterize Northumbrian, and another name to those amongst the four dialects which make up Old English, so we can group Old English with a number of other languages of much the same time—they include Old Saxon, Old High German, Old Norse, and Gothic—as 'Germanic'. Nor was the Germanic an independent family of languages: its regular similarities with others, including Latin, Greek, Sanskrit, the Slavonic languages, and Celtic, justify a place for Germanic along with them as a collateral descendant from a language which we believe was spoken some four or five thousand years ago, perhaps not far from Lithuania; this language, whose features we can only infer, we call Indo-European. (On the similarities, see the last chapter.)

The strangeness of a page of Old English when we see it today arises in part from its employment of a number of letters no longer in our alphabet. The word *æt* is the same in sound, spelling and meaning as our word 'at', and so *þæt* or *ðæt* are substantially the same as 'that' (*þ* and *ð* both represented the sound we spell as 'th'; another form for 'w', and different shapes for a few other letters, do not appear so frequently in modern editions of Old English texts). The real strangeness, however, is in less superficial differences between Old English and our present-day language, differences that have come about through changes in the sounds of words (as when *bāt* came to be pronounced 'boat'), in the shapes of words (as when *hlāford* was progressively simplified to 'lord'), in the way words were handled in sentences (as when *mannum* came to be phrased 'to the men'), in the actual words used (as when *þēow* was replaced by 'servant').

In the ninth-century translation of Bede's *Ecclesiastical History* we find:

> *Þeossum wordum gelīcum ōðre aldormen ond ðæs cyninges geþeaht- eras spræcon.*
> 'The other aldermen and the king's councillors spoke in words like unto these.'

Some words (*ōðre, aldormen*) have changed in little but the letters used to spell them and in details of pronunciation: the Old English would have been something like 'AHLdermen', 'OHther'. Some (*cyninges*, 'king's') have been simplified. To show the role of the phrase 'words like ... these' we add prepositions, '*in* words like *unto* these'. The Old English employs the ending -*um* to relate the phrase to the rest of the sentence (but we still use the ending -*s*, 'the king's', 'of the king', to show 'possession', and the same ending, 'councillors'—*geþeahteras*—to show plurality). And the word *geþeahtere* itself has been replaced by 'councillor': the Old English word is from another which survives in our word 'thought', so that it meant something like 'deliberator'.

In present-day English, 'spoke' might follow 'he' or 'they'—it might have a singular or a plural subject. In Old English, the ending -*on* of *spræcon* shows that it is plural. The only plural noun beside 'councillors' and 'aldermen' is 'words'; the only plural pronoun is 'these'. But we have seen that the ending -*um* shows that we should read '*in* words', '*unto* these'—that they cannot be the subject of 'spoke', even though plural. In this way, the endings of Old English words, nouns and verbs alike, served to relate the words to one another. Most of these endings, we have noted, are now lost; to express the same relationships, we depend on prepositions and on word-order. Old English is relatively sparing in the use of prepositions, and relatively free in the use of word-order.

These features of Old English are reflected in the literary styles of the period. Consider the following part of a short poem, once again from the translation of Bede:

Nū sculon herigean	*heofonrīces Weard,*
Now (we) must praise	heaven-land's Guardian,
Meotodes meahte	*ond His mōdgeþanc,*
(The) Lord's might	and His mind-thought,
weorc Wuldorfæder,	*swā Hē wundra gehwæs,*
(The) work of the Glory-	as He of wonders of each,
father,	
ēce Drihten,	*ōr onstealde.*
(The) eternal Lord,	(the) beginning created.

'Now we must praise the Guardian of the kingdom of Heaven, the Lord's might and His intention, the work of the glorious Father, as He, the eternal Lord, created the beginning of each one of wonders.'

You will have noticed that in the third line the present-day English version has resorted to a number of prepositions to do the work that word-endings did in Old English. Even so, the word-order is so strange to us that a word-for-word translation makes little sense of the line. But to the Old English audience, there would have been no such problems in understanding the poem. They would have been able to admire the way the poet made use of his freedom of word-order to interlace the words in each line in a fixed pattern of alliteration, where the first *stressed* syllable in the second part of each line (*heofon-, mōd-, wundra, ōr*) set the alliterative scheme of the line into which at least one stressed word in the first half line had to fit (any vowel alliterated with any other). They would have admired the variation of the important ideas by apposition within the grammatical pattern, so that, for example, the verb 'praise' has *four* direct objects: 'Guardian', 'might', 'intention', 'work'. And they would have admired the inventive use of compound words like 'heaven-land', 'mind-thought', 'Glory-father'. All these features of Old English poetic diction are interdependent . . . the alliterative demand and the taste for apposition can best be satisfied within a free word-order, and the use of compounds serves them both . . . and they all capitalize on the conditions of contemporary Old English grammar and vocabulary, that is, they are shaped by the linguistic resources of their own day. They were traditional, but by no means stilted; we find them strange only by the same measure that the language in which they are written is strange.

Because of the close connexion between Old English poetic diction and Old English language at large, its devices were almost equally viable in prose: perhaps at no period in English literature have poetic form and prose form so closely approached each other. To stay for our example with the vernacular versions of Bede, here is a prose paraphrase by Ælfric, eleventh-century abbot of Eynsham, of a portion of the *Ecclesiastical History*:

> *Sē fērde on his iugoðe fram his frēondum and māgum tō*
> He fared in his youth from his friends and kinsmen to
> *Scotlande on sǣ, and þǣr sōna wearð gefullod and*
> Ireland by sea, and there soon was baptized and
> *his gefēran samod þe mid him sīþedon.*
> his companions together who with him voyaged.

Here rhythm and alliteration combine to produce an effect very like that of Old English poetry, and some editors have printed it as such; but the devices of poetry are not the forms of poetry, and this example is prose, even though of a high artistic order.

Old English, then, was not a new language, but merely the first stage of the growth of English in England. It was a Germanic language, depending on word-endings to a great extent to show the relationships between words in sentences, and (somewhat like modern German) capable of building its vocabulary from its own resources, as when it derived *geþeahtere* from 'thought' or compounded *heofon* with *rīc*. These features underlie many of its most characteristic literary techniques, both in prose and in poetry.

For Further Reading

ABOUT OLD ENGLISH LANGUAGE:

R. C. Alston, *An Introduction to Old English*, 1961.
L. Blakeley, *Teach Yourself Old English*, 1964.
G. L. Brook, *An Introduction to Old English*, 1955.
R. E. Diamond, *Old English Grammar and Reader*, 1970.
C. B. Heiatt, *Essentials of Old English*, 1968.
R. J. Kispert, *Old English: An Introduction*, 1971.
B. Mitchell, *A Guide to Old English*, 1965.
S. Moore and T. A. Knott, *The Elements of Old English*, 1955.
R. Quirk and C. L. Wrenn, *An Old English Grammar*, 1958.
A. S. C. Ross, *The Essentials of Anglo-Saxon Grammar*, 1954.

ABOUT OLD ENGLISH LITERATURE:

G. K. Anderson, *The Literature of the Anglo-Saxons*, 1949.
S. B. Greenfield, *A Critical History of Old English Literature*, 1965.
C. L. Wrenn, *A Study of Old English Literature*, 1967.

COLLECTIONS OF OLD ENGLISH LITERATURE:

W. F. Bolton, *An Old English Anthology*, 1965.
J. W. Bright, *An Anglo-Saxon Reader*, 1951.
R. Fowler, *Old English Prose and Verse*, 1966.
H. Sweet, *An Anglo-Saxon Reader*, 1967.
P. S. Ardern, *First Readings in Old English*, 1951.

CHAPTER TWO

Middle English

As all languages change, so did Old English. We have already seen that the diversification of dialects later in the period cannot be accounted for merely by the tribal origins of the settlers. Moreover, some of the forms we have been studying were involved in notable changes. The recorded word *hlāford*, for example, descended from an earlier unrecorded Old English compound of the *heofon* plus *rīc* type, *hlāf* plus *weard*, 'guardian of the loaf', and *hlāford* itself is a middle stage in the process of simplification which led to present-day English 'lord'. Word-endings like *-um* and *-on*, which were never stressed, both became a sound something like '-unh', and some late Old English manuscripts show it by not distinguishing between them in spelling. This change is a change in the sound of words, but of course it reduces the ability of endings to signal the place of a word in the sentence, and so eventually changes the system of signals. And no doubt Continental influences, particularly in the courts of Cnut and Ethelred, introduced some non-English and even non-Germanic words into the language, although very few of these have survived. Probably the writers of the manuscripts were conservative men who did not approve of foreign words in important documents, any more than the writers of court circulars employ the 'Americanisms' current in England today.

When we talk about the characteristics of Middle English that distinguish it from Old English, then, we must recognize that none of them appeared as an overnight consequence of the Norman Conquest, and indeed that many of them had been continuing features of change in Old English. But the Norman Conquest had consequences that accelerated a number of these changes, and in the long run brought others to light. For a long time after the Conquest, the place of English as a language for official and literary use was taken by Latin and French. The place that English, and particularly West Saxon, had held in these uses during the Anglo-Saxon period had led to a conservatism in the written vernacular. We have noted how this conservatism influenced the vocabulary of surviving documents. It probably influenced the spelling too: the blending of -*um* and -*on* in writing must have taken place long after it had become a common feature of the spoken language. And changes in the shape of words and sentences doubtless took place more rapidly in speech than in formal writing. All these discrepancies are to be seen, in a way, in the present-day gulf between official and literary writing on the one hand and our ordinary speech on the other. (Would anyone ever *say* the sentence I have just written?)

At the end of the domination of Latin and French for formal use, the kind of use that went into the documents that survive for our study, the English that we find has been changing freely as any language will, and absorbing the influences of the Norman Conquest. At an early stage the changes and influences are not so marked. Just over a century after the Conquest, a writer in or near the area of the previous West Saxon dialect wrote:

> *Þah cleannesse of chasteté ne beo nawt bune ed Godd,*
> Though purity of   chastity is no purchase from God,
>> *ah beo geove of grace, ungraciuse stondeð þer togeines*
> but is given out of grace, ungraciously (they) stand
>>>>>>>> there against
>> *and makieð ham unwurðe to halden se heh þing,*
> and make themselves unworthy to hold so high (a) thing,
>> *þe nulleð swinc þervore bliðeliche þolien.*
> who will not effort for it joyfully suffer.
>>>>>>> (*Ancrene Wisse*, Part VI)

Once again the strangeness of the letters and the spelling make this seem very far from our present-day language, and indeed many features are still like Old English. The writer freely uses **a**

double negative (*ne beo nawt*) to do the work of single negative,
a characteristic of early English that continued to Shakespeare's
time and beyond. He uses words for which we would always
(*þolien*, 'suffer') or usually (*cleannesse*, 'purity') substitute one of
Latin or French origin. He puts the infinitive at the end of the
clause instead of soon after 'will not'. Most important of all, he
does not need to write '*they* stand' because the ending *-eð* (*stondeð*,
makieð, *nulleð*) is still available to show that the subject of the verb
is plural—in this case present plural, just as in Old English *-on*
showed that a verb was past plural.

Most written language is more conservative than spoken
language, and some sorts of written language, like the religious
instruction from which this passage is taken, are especially so.
Moreover, the same book was translated into both Latin and
French for English audiences, probably because some still
doubted the adequacy of English for such sorts of writing.

But the real changes have taken place all the same. Against
the survival of *cleannesse* and *þolien* we must consider the new
words from the French, *chasteté, grace, ungraciuse*; against the reten-
tion of some older verb-endings we must consider the loss of
some others and of noun-endings (Old English would have had
to *haldenne*, *æt Gode*); against the infinitive at the end of the
sentence we must consider the otherwise 'modern' appearance
of the word-order and the reliance on prepositions (*of, ed*). We
should be justified in saying that in these ways the sentence is
transitional. It is transitional as well in style, for its organization
depends not so much on the devices borrowed from poetry that
characterized much that was best in Old English prose, but rather
on the careful order and balance of the clauses. The writer has
put his subordinate clause first; balanced it by another; introduced
his major clause (linking it with the foregoing by the echo of
grace/ungraciuse), and balanced it again with another; and rounded
off with a final subordinate clause, whose subject, however, was
implied in the major clauses. The 'normal' order for such a
sentence might have been 'People who will not . . . suffer,

ungraciously stand against grace, and make themselves un-
worthy . . . , although (of course) chastity is not purchased from
God, but given out of grace.' By reversing the order, the author
has saved himself numerous repetitions, and he has given force
to his argument by saving the most important word, 'suffer',
to the end; and of course he has made the sentence more interesting. Many of these aspects of his style, as we have seen, are
directly evolved from the particular transitional state of English
around the year 1200.

When we turn to the late Middle English period, we find in
Chaucer

> 'Beth war, I prey yow; for, by hevene kyng,
> Ful many a man weneth to seen a thyng,
> And it is al another than it semeth.
> He that mysconceyveth, he mysdemeth.'
>   (*Merchant's Tale*, 2407–10)

The passage is not Chaucer's best-known, nor his most French
in style or vocabulary. But even here the French element is
significant: it appears in a conservative phrase like 'I *pray* you'
(compare modern French *je vous en prie*), and it enters freely into
combination with native English words, for while *mysdemeth* is
pure English (*mis-* plus *deem*, 'judge'), *mysconceyveth* is a mixture
of English *mis-* plus French *conceive*, the whole thing rounded
off with an English verb-ending. The French words in Chaucer,
then, have not the status of those we studied in the transitional
prose text. The earlier writer uses them perhaps with a sense of
their foreignness and specialness; they are available to him as
English words, but mainly in special uses—in this case, the
technical vocabulary of theology. But for Chaucer they have
become part of the material of the language, to be woven freely
into his fabric. Many words we use today come to us from Latin,
either directly or—more often—through French. How many
depends on where you choose to look: the dictionary is not an
appropriate book, because not everyone uses all of it constantly.

But, for example, there are four such borrowings in the previous sentence: 'depends', 'dictionary', 'appropriate', 'constantly', a verb, noun, adjective and adverb. It is in these parts of speech that we meet French words most often: in prepositions, articles, pronouns, and conjunctions there are almost none. (Of course other languages made a contribution as well: our modern sentence 'They take their seats with their fellows' is entirely, except for the native preposition 'with', made up of loan-words from Old Norse.)

Before we leave Chaucer, we should take note of some other aspects of his language. For the first time, I have not supplied a translation. This is partly because Chaucer's is the most recent text we have looked at, and so the nearest to our present-day language. But it is also partly because Chaucer's English lies almost directly behind our own; that is, the language most of us speak is descended from a dialect of English like his. For there continued to be dialect divisions in the Middle English period, rather more than in the Old English period; and some of them are collateral relations of Chaucer's English and hence not directly related to ours. Some texts, indeed, even of Chaucer's day, look very different from what we have seen of him.

> *Þay bowen bi bonkkes þer boghes ar bare,*
> They   passed by banks where boughs are bare
> *Þay clomben bi clyffes þer clenges þe colde.*
> They   climbed by cliffs where clings the cold.
> *Þe heven wats up halt, bot ugly þer under—*
> The heaven was drawn up, but ugly thereunder—
> *Mist muged on þe mor, malt on þe mountes.*
> Mist drizzled on the moor, melted on the mountains.
>   (*Sir Gawain and the Green Knight*, 2077–80)

As you can see, little more than the spelling is unfamiliar here, and the two strangest words (*bowen, muged*) have present-day English descendants: 'bow', 'to bend onesself', which also used to mean 'to bend one's way', 'to go'; and 'muggy', 'damp', which shows up in a different part of speech and on a less formal level. The anonymous poet treats 'climb' as a strong verb like 'win', with *i* in the present and *o* in the past, and he treats 'melt' in much the same way. As the translation shows, we now treat these and a great many others as weak, simply adding *-ed* to the end rather than changing the vowel: our poet shows that he regarded *muged* as such a weak verb.

He also retains the *-on* ending for the past plural, here softened to *-en*, and like Chaucer, he has a special ending for the present singular in the third person, although Chaucer uses the older *-eth* (*weneth, semeth*, etc.) where the poet of the north-west midlands has used *-s* (*clenges*). Although the two forms continued well into the seventeenth century, Chaucer's thereafter became increasingly restricted to special, notably religious uses ('He maketh me to walk . . .'). This is an uncharacteristic example of a dialect difference where Chaucer's dialect did not prevail; but the decision came long after Chaucer's day.

There is little left in the way of signals in the noun-endings except for the plural (*bonkkes, boghes, clyffes, mountes*) which we retain today along with the possessive singular, not represented in these selections. Chaucer's *hevene kyng* reveals a possessive plural softened from Old English *-a* (compare *wundra*, 'of wonders', p. 4, and *Ancrene Wisse*, 'Guide of Anchorites'), but it is in a highly conventional phrase, a fossil survival hardly characteristic of the language of his day.

Both poets use prepositions freely, and—it is almost a corollary —their word-order, even though this is poetry, seems most natural to us. But their verse form is another matter. Like so much in those four lines, Chaucer's versification seems familiar: rhymed couplets made up of ten syllables alternating unstressed and stressed. There is a good deal of variation, but this is clearly the iambic pentameter line that, in rhymed or unrhymed forms, has been the staple of English poets ever since (the rhyming iambic pentameter couplets were Chaucer's introduction from the French). Not so the poet of the second passage. If his verse

form is at all familiar, it is because you have studied the last
chapter carefully. Like the poet whose work we considered on
p. 4, this one makes alliteration, not rhyme, his unifying
element, and instead of counting all the syllables in the line, as
Chaucer does, he counts only the main stresses, allowing four to
each verse. Chaucer, then, stands at the beginning of a long
tradition of verse unified by rhyme and scanned by feet; the
anonymous poet stands at the end of a tradition of verse unified
by alliteration and scanned by stress. Working as they did at
much the same time, with the language at the same stage of its
history, in verse little differentiated by dialect but very greatly
differentiated by poetic form, they achieved to a remarkably
equal degree the assimilation of highly similar linguistic resources
into highly divergent poetic idioms.

In Middle English, then, the Germanic word-stock of Old
English remained undisturbed in some parts of speech, but was
changed with increasing rapidity in some others, chiefly by
borrowing from the French brought by the Norman Conquest.
At the same time other changes, which had begun before the
Conquest, were accelerated, so that many important word-ending
signals were softened or blended, and many others disappeared
entirely, with consequent new signals, particularly in word-order
and the use of prepositions, coming to do the same job. The
altered aspect of this stage of the language, although it is only
part of a continuous change, justifies a new name for it.

For Further Reading

ABOUT MIDDLE ENGLISH LANGUAGE:

K. Brunner, *An Outline of Middle English Grammar*, 1963.
J. W. Clark, *Early English*, 1967.
J. Fisiak, *A Short Grammar of Middle English*, 1968.
H. Kökeritz, *A Guide to Chaucer's Pronunciation*, 1962.
F. Mossé, *A Handbook of Middle English*, 1952.
M. M. Roseborough, *An Outline of Middle English Grammar*, 1970.
E. E. Wardale, *An Introduction to Middle English*, 1937.

ABOUT MIDDLE ENGLISH LITERATURE:

B. Cottle, *The Triumph of English, 1350–1400*, 1969.
G. Kane, *Middle English Literature*, 1951.
R. M. Wilson, *Early Middle English Literature*, 1939.

COLLECTIONS OF MIDDLE ENGLISH LITERATURE:

J. A. W. Bennett, G. V. Smithers and N. Davis, *Early Middle English Verse and Prose*, 1966.
B. Dickins and R. M. Wilson, *Early Middle English Texts*, 1956.
O. F. Emerson, *A Middle English Reader*, 1950.
K. Sisam, *Fourteenth Century Verse and Prose*, 1955.

CHAPTER THREE

Early Modern English

The Old English prose on p. 5 was written near the year 1000;
the Middle English prose on p. 8 was written about 1200; the
Middle English verse on pp. 10 and 11 was written just before
1400. Just after 1600 Shakespeare wrote

> Everything that heard him play,
> Even the billowes of the sea. . . .
> *(Henry VIII, III.i)*

In this last, as in each of the examples, we note a great change in
the language over the interval of 200 years. But Shakespeare's
language appears entirely familiar to us, although it is almost
400 years old; the spelling, the vocabulary, the shapes of the words
and the phrases seem to have changed but little in that time.
Why? Did our language cease to change after his day? To answer
that question, we must go back to Chaucer for a moment. He
wrote,

> 'Now', *quod oure Hoost*, 'yit lat *me* talke *to the.*
> *Why artow so* discoloured of *thy face?'*
> *(Canon's Yeoman's Prol.,* 663–4)

Chaucer's pronunciations of the italicized words would have been
something like this: *face*, 'fahs'; *me*, *the*, 'may', 'thay'; *why*, *thy*,
'whee', 'thee'; *quod*, *hoost*, *so*, 'qᵘawd', 'hawst', 'saw'; *to*, 'toe';
artow, *now*, *oure*, 'artoo', 'noo', 'oor'. This change of the sounds of
six vowels took place over a long period of time, starting soon
after Chaucer wrote and still incomplete in a few details in Shakespeare's day. You can see that it is a very profound change, that

indeed if you read the two lines with the suggested pronunciations, the great difference between present-day English and fourteenth-century English will stand out as it hardly does on the printed page. For whereas the change between Old English and Middle English involves chiefly the vocabulary and the shapes of words and sentences, the change between Middle English and Modern English involves chiefly the pronunciation, and involves it in a way the spelling hardly shows. The change of the six vowels which is the most important part of this change in pronunciation is called the Great Vowel Shift.

Returning to the Shakespeare couplet, we note that the rhyme appears to be false. But before we decide that it is, we should recall the vowel shift from 'may', 'thay' to 'me', 'thee', and some inconsistencies in modern spelling like 'dear/bear', 'freak/break', even 'Keats/Yeats'. It will appear from this evidence that the spelling for these words was fixed before the vowel shift began, and that the spelling did not change to take account of the shift. The shift was not complete in Shakespeare's time, and in our own it is not represented in some words: but we can reason that Shakespeare pronounced 'sea' as we would 'say', and that this rhyme is not false.

So the familiar spellings of Chaucer's 'now', 'to', 'me', 'so', 'why', 'thy', 'face', all represent unfamiliar—indeed, profoundly different—pronunciations, and although the sounds had changed by Shakespeare's day and have continued to change since then until ours, the spelling has remained remarkably stable. The main reason for this stability lies in the invention that reached England almost exactly halfway between Chaucer's death (1400) and Shakespeare's birth (1564), the printing press. We have already noted that the establishment of West Saxon in the later Old English period had the effect of giving the written language an increasingly uniform and constant character, so that official and literary documents less and less represented the state of the current spoken language. This effect is bound to follow when there is an 'established' variety of the language in general written use, for although this variety is of course derived from the spoken language, it soon develops its own rules, and these rules constitute a standard to which the written language can be kept. The spoken language, which by its nature is immune to regulation, continues to change, and the written standard becomes more and more distant from it to the same degree that the written language keeps to its hard-and-fast rules. This is truest of spelling, but it is true in some measure for the shapes of words and of sentences as well, and we all reserve some parts of our vocabulary for speech alone and others for writing alone, no matter how many words appear in both.

The beginning of printing in England, only a few years after its invention in Europe, had the effect of creating a demand for a standard written English. William Caxton (1422?–1491), who introduced printing around 1477, himself complained that

our langage now used varyeth ferre from that, whiche was used and spoken whan I was borne. For we englysshe men ben borne under the domynacyon of the mone, whiche is never stedfaste, but ever waverynge, wexynge one season and waneth and dyscreaseth another season. And that comyn englysshe that is spoken in one shyre varyeth from a nother.... Loo what sholde a man in thyse dayes now wryte, 'egges' or 'eyren'? Certaynly it is harde to playse every man, by cause of dyversité and chaunge of langage.

(Prologue to *Eneydos*)

Caxton is pointing to two aspects of linguistic diversity, that is diversity in time and diversity in space, difference from one age to another and from one place to another. An important advantage of widespread use of written language is that it overcomes both time and space, extending language beyond the moment and range of speech. And the really widespread use of written language was not possible until the age of printing. When it came, it drew attention to the diversity of the spoken language

which, if it had been reflected in printing, would have thwarted
the great advantage printing had to offer.

Amongst the books Caxton printed was Chaucer's *House of
Fame*, in the Epilogue to which Caxton said of Chaucer,

> in alle hys werkys he excellyth in myn oppynyon alle
> other wryters in our Englyssh. . . . For of hym alle other
> have borowed syth and taken in alle theyr wel sayeng and
> wrytyng.

Chaucer, for Caxton, was a model from the recent past (Chaucer
died only twenty-two years before Caxton was born) whose
works set the pattern for all conscientious writers: so important
was the pattern, indeed, that having published an edition of the
Canterbury Tales, Caxton published a second edition when a
better manuscript became available to him. Little wonder then
that Caxton and other early printers turned to manuscripts of
Chaucer and of Chaucer's age when they sought for their own
pattern for 'wel wrytyng'. In this way Caxton avoided the
confused linguistic situation of his own day, the choice between
'egges' and 'eyren', and took as his model an earlier writer of
acknowledged authority and reputation. Chaucer's English—and
notably his spellings—took on the role of linguistic standard
because of his literary excellence, and sound-changes that had
taken place since his time were simply ignored.

Of course Chaucer's spellings are not exactly Shakespeare's,
nor yet again ours; but setting aside punctuation as a matter
separate from spelling, and concentrating on the printed forms
of the written language, we can still say that spelling was by and
large stabilized by the time Shakespeare was born, and that the
standard of stability was the literary dialect of London English
exemplified by and descended from Chaucer.

The coming of the printing press had another effect during the
years in which Shakespeare lived and wrote, an effect on the
vocabulary of English. Of course the vocabulary of English had
been changing, as we have seen, from its earliest recorded history.

But the character of these changes differed from one age to the next. In Middle English, especially after 1250 or so, a large number of French words entered the vocabulary. They were preeminently words to do with those aspects of life which the Norman conquerors had taken over from or introduced to the vanquished Anglo-Saxons, notably the law, the military, high society, beaux arts, administration, religion, and learning. The lines from Chaucer on p. 15 display a number of them: 'host', 'discoloured', 'face'. But even though such language entered by way of the ruling classes and their characteristic interests, it was not a language that was limited to them in application, as the three examples from Chaucer show. The massive intake of French vocabulary in Middle English was so great precisely because much of it had to do with the language of every-day life, and it rapidly became part of common speech, particularly when French itself ceased to be widely spoken amongst the upper classes.

After the Middle English period, however, and especially after the introduction of printing, the main sorts of innovation in English vocabulary change. The innovations become less a matter of natural linguistic borrowing, and more a matter of deliberate addition to the vocabulary; and they are less to do with every-day life, and more to do with literature, philosophy and other subjects where the printed book is an object of interest in its own right. As a result, words enter the vocabulary of common speech through the familiarity that literature has given them, where before literature tended rather to base its vocabulary on the resources of common speech. In so far as the spoken language is 'natural' and the written one 'artificial', the new situation is one in which nature imitates art. In bringing this relationship about, the printed book, and the wide increase in literacy which it made possible, played a major role.

Shortly after Caxton, writers began to complain of more shortcomings of literary English than just the instability in space and time that worried him. Their remarks are properly the subject of chapter 6, but John Skelton (1460?–1529), a poet whose use of English Caxton had praised, may suffice to illustrate them here:

> 'Our naturall tong is rude,
> And hard to be enneude
> With pullysshed termes lusty;
> Our language is so rusty,
> So cankered and so full
> Of frowardes, and so dull,
> That if I wolde apply
> To wryte ornatly,
> I wot not where to fynd
> Termes to serve my mynde.'
>
> (*Booke of Phyllyp Sparowe*, 769–78)

Skelton is complaining of the poverty of English 'terms', that is, the special words of learned subjects and high style, even though he has benefited richly from the French inheritance: of the 48 words in this passage, fully a quarter are of French origin, and the largest part of the remainder is from the strongholds of native vocabulary, prepositions, pronouns, and conjunctions. Skelton, in short, is a part of the linguistic tradition which Caxton and the early printers had confirmed; he is linguistically 'main stream', and his remarks must be judged as such.

For the 'terms' which they felt were needed to make English literature flexible and ornate, Skelton and the sixteenth century turned to languages of established reputation, first to Latin and Greek, later to the earlier monuments of English itself. Other modern languages, notably French, continued to make their contribution: of an average 1000 French borrowings in English, over half had been made by the time Chaucer died, and the century of heaviest borrowing thereafter is the sixteenth, in which a further 18 per cent. appeared (in the fifteenth century, the figure is under 15 per cent.; in the seventeenth century, it is down to 10 per cent.) So in Spenser's *Faerie Queene* we find

'Me ill besits, that in der-doing armes,
And honour's suit my vowed dayes do spend,
Unto thy bounteous baytes, and pleasing charmes,
With which weake men thou witchest, to attend:
Regard of worldly mucke doth fowly blend,
And low abase the high heroicke spright,
That joyes for crownes and kingdomes to contend;
Faire shields, gay steedes, bright armes be my delight:
Those be the riches fit for an advent'rous knight.'

(Book II, vii.10)

The passage is a mixture of the old, the new, and the old in new forms or meanings. Old, of course, are the grammatical 'bones' of the sentence, the pronouns, articles, conjunctions and prepositions, and parts of the verbs *be* and *do*: this class accounts for 28 of the 70 words in the stanza. Also old are the words from Old English and Middle English, including borrowings from French already part of the language in Caxton's day: these account for a further 34 words. But 8 words—almost one in every line, on average—have made their first appearance in the sixteenth century, or at any rate their first appearance in this meaning or form.

New words altogether are *der-doing, heroicke, contend*. The first is an invention of Spenser's, derived from the noun *derring-do* (*Faerie Queene*, II.iv.42, VI.v.37; *Shepherd's Calendar*, Oct.65, Dec.43). It rests on his reading of the 14th-poet Lydgate, who wrote that Troilus was noble in 'dorryng do' knightly feats, that is, in 'daring to do' them; but Spenser took the phrase to mean 'deeds of valour', and his sixteenth-century edition of Lydgate contained the misprint 'derrynge do'. Ben Jonson once said that 'Spenser, in affecting the ancients, writ no language', and the observation is nowhere more true than here, where the poet's eagerness to enrich his diction with old terms has made him overlook the misprint and his misunderstanding alike.

Heroicke and *contend* both come from the Latin, the former ultimately from the Greek. *Heroicke* first appears in English about 1549. *Contend* appears earlier, in 1514, with the meaning 'struggle'; but its meaning here, 'compete, vie', is not recorded before 1589, the year before Spenser published his poem. Both words are sixteenth-century innovations, and the sense in which Spenser used *contend* was especially new.

New meanings likewise account for two other innovations in the stanza. One is *witch*, here meaning 'charm, entice' instead of its older intransitive sense, 'practise witchcraft'. It is a shortened form of *bewitch*, first used in this sense in 1526; it makes its first appearance without *be-* in this stanza. The other innovation appears to be *suit*. It can mean 'following, retinue', and this meaning is recorded in Middle English: but it seems that it really means 'pursuit', the 'pursuit of honour', in which case this is the first recorded use in that sense.

Finally there are three words which appear here in forms which are distinctively sixteenth century. One such is *spright*, another form of *sprite* (from *spirit*), first noticed in this spelling in 1533; it shows the influence of native words in *-ight* like *wight*. Another similar instance is *delight*, which comes from a Middle English word spelled *delite* (from the same word as *delicious*), and the sixteenth-century spelling seems to arise from a mistaken association with *light*. The earlier spelling continued to the end of the sixteenth century, but the new one prevailed. The last example, *advent'rous*, comes from French *aventure* by way of a Middle English *aventerous*. The Latin source of the French word, *adventura*, influenced the French spelling in the fifteenth century, and Caxton occasionally uses it. Presumably the pronunciation did not adapt itself to the 'reformed' spelling immediately, for *aventure* appears—in a translation of Virgil, which we should expect to be aware of Latin sources—as late as 1583, but once again the innovation prevailed. In all three cases the sixteenth-century spelling is a literary one, based on ideas about the history of the word rather than on current pronunciation.

Writing at the close of the first 1000 years of the English language, Spenser employs words, forms or meanings which are new to his century in more than 11 per cent. of the stanza. Borrowed words, revived words, new meanings for current words, all served to enrich the literature of sixteenth-century English, even though the innovations included a number of mistakes and irrelevancies. The changes of spelling might suggest that spelling was not yet settled, but the reverse is true: *sprite*, *delite* and *aventure* could be respelled as they were precisely because spelling had already become so distant from pronunciation that it could adjust its 'rules' independently, and this distance, as we have seen, is a feature of stability in spelling. By the end of the sixteenth century the transition from medieval to modern English was substantially complete in the literary dialect, a dialect which had assumed an identity and a role of its own. Henceforth the influence of the spoken language on the written would no longer be a one-way matter, and forms of mainly literary origin would increasingly influence those of everyday speech.

For Further Reading

E. J. Dobson, *English Pronunciation, 1500–1700*, 1968.
H. Kökeritz, *Shakespeare's Pronunciation*, 1953.
G. P. Krapp, rev. A. H. Marckwardt, *Modern English*, 1969.
G. H. McKnight, *Modern English in the Making*, 1956.
A. C. Partridge, *Tudor to Augustan English*, 1969.
M. Schlauch, *The English Language in Modern Times*, 1959.

CHAPTER FOUR

Late Modern English

The relative stability of literary English since the sixteenth century
has had two effects on students of the literature. One is to have
implied a kind of discontinuity in language and literature alike
between the Renaissance and the age immediately before it, so
that the sixteenth century seems much of a piece with our own
age, but the fifteenth and earlier centuries very alien. No doubt the
fact of the printing press, and even more of the other technological
advances of which it was only one, influenced the sensibility of
literate society, and to this extent we really are more akin to the
sixteenth century than to the middle ages. But many of the
consequences of printing that heighten this sense of kinship are
very superficial, and the relegation of medieval literature to a
specialist or minority place in literary studies results from a
misunderstanding of linguistic history.

The second effect has been a kind of overconfidence, for if
students of the literature have been unrealistically disinclined
to carry their studies further back than 1500, they have also been
too inclined to look upon texts written since then as though
written in their own language. But the change of language is
continuous, if not steady, and a linguistic misjudgement here too
is a risk of literary misjudgement.

The greatest change has been in the meaning of words. When
Ben Jonson wrote 'they (in night Of their ambition) [will] not
perceive the traine, Till, in the ingine, they are caught, and slaine'
(*Sejanus*, 1603, II, 267–9), he unintentionally laid a trap for the
unwary reader three hundred or more years later. For Jonson
'train' could mean 'ruse', from the French word meaning 'to

24

draw'; that is, something that draws, not only something that can be drawn. And 'engine' (which he spelled to show its derivation from Latin *ingenium*, 'invention', source of our 'ingenious') could mean any device to procure a result, including a scheme, something very like 'train'. When the technology of the nineteenth century produced steam locomotion, the language, as often before and since, was called upon to name something which previously had not existed. In this case it already had the resources to supply some of the new nomenclature, and the words 'train' and 'engine' took on additional senses developed out of those they already had (even though the new ones were no longer, in the railroad context, capable of meaning the same thing). But the new meanings are capable of making sense in Jonson's lines, and if we did not know that there were no railroads in his day, we should risk—in careless reading at least—seriously misunderstanding what he wrote. Not all words change their meanings this way, but the peril of misunderstanding an early Modern English literary text because of unnoticed changes of meaning remains great.

Just as new meanings did not account for all the sixteenth-century innovations in the stanza from Spenser on p. 21, so too they do not account for all the changes that have taken place since then. New words have continued to enter English from foreign languages, and new coinages have been made. To mention only the languages from which English had already been borrowing for centuries, French was the source of 'police' and 'invalid', Latin of 'locomotive', Greek and Latin of 'television'. But these borrowings represent no new development in English vocabulary-building, as the thoroughly assimilated Middle English 'gentleman' (French plus English) or more recent 'unable' (English plus French) both illustrate, along with thousands of others; nor were they so numerous as in early Modern English and before. Compounds from native or naturalized words like 'lighthouse' or 'windscreen' have come into being with the things they refer to. Yet once again it would be wrong to concentrate on these innovations as if they were part of a wholesale transformation of the vocabulary such as those that took place between the Norman Conquest and 1600. A conversation or a book on a specialized subject like automobiles or electronics will contain many of them, particularly if the subject is a new one; but the vocabulary of an older, even though equally specialized, subject like navigation will contain far fewer, and non-technical prose and poetry very few indeed. The 'central' vocabulary of a novel, a poem, or for that matter a leading editorial, can easily be entirely composed of words three hundred years old at the youngest without betraying an air of ancientness; yet the 'ancients' Spenser was accused of affecting were most of them not so old as that.

What is true of the language in time is also true of the language in space. Since Spenser wrote, the English language has ceased to be the tongue of an island off the shore of Europe, spoken by perhaps four million people, and has become one on which the sun never sets, with almost a hundred native speakers for every one in 1600. The literature of English, even within Britain, has by means of near-universal education, social changes, and the greatly reduced cost of books, ceased to be the avocation of a small privileged class and become the common companion of almost everyone who speaks its language—particularly if we class newspapers and light novels as 'literature'. Both nationally and internationally, then, literary English addresses itself to a wide variety of readers, whose own speech is perhaps the point of greatest diversity amongst them. Yet just as an editorial of 1966 looks little different from one of 1666, so a novel written in London looks much like one written in Edinburgh, New York or Brisbane. Some forms may differ, but they differ unimportantly: 'labor' is an American spelling, but it does not represent a distinctively American pronunciation in a way that 'labour' can not. 'Photo' is not a usual form in America, but if heard there it would probably sound like 'FOH-doh'. In some parts of London it would be 'FOW-tow' (rhyming with 'allow'), in others almost

'FEH-teh'. Some speakers would replace the 't' with a catch of the breath in the throat ('glottal stop'); all would observe a difference between the word pronounced on its own and the word in derivatives like 'photographer'. Yet the spelling is still the same. In this way literary English remains subject to the same arbitrary 'rules' throughout the world, and—as a medium for reading and writing—retains a degree of universal intelligibility both in the content of its vocabulary and in its spelling that Caxton would surely have envied.

The stability we see in vocabulary and spelling also regulates the shapes of words and of sentences. In the 1611 translation of the Bible we read 'Lovest thou me?' (*John* 21, 16), and the example appears to contradict what I have just said. But examples in isolation can be misleading. For one thing, the Bible, along with certain other kinds of religious writing, employs a diction traditionally very conservative: the phrase in question appeared over six hundred years earlier as *'Lufast þu me?'*, that is, with differences in pronunciation and spelling, but with the same two features that seem so strange to us now, the word-order (instead of 'do you love me?') and the use of 'thou' (along with its associated verb-ending, '-est'). For another thing, these two features are amongst the relatively few fundamental ones that distinguish our handling of words and sentences from that of 1611.

'Lovest thou me?' has three words, 'do you love me?' four. The extra word is 'do', and we use it now in four important ways: in a question, like 'do you love me?'; in a negative, like 'you do not love me' (for earlier 'you love me not'); in a negative imperative, like 'do not love me!' (for earlier 'love me not!'); and for emphasis, like 'I *do* love you'. When the verb in the clause is 'be', 'have' or one of verbs that do not take '-s' after 'he' in the present (like 'can', 'will', 'must', etc.), 'do' is not employed ('do you love?', but 'are you?', 'can you?'). Since this exception applies to all four major uses, we can assume that they are closely connected. In the first three, 'do' obviously takes the position in

the sentence taken by the verb 'love' (or whatever) in the earlier
ways of putting it (and taken even now by 'be', 'have', 'can' and
the rest), and the other words change their positions. The same
is true of the fourth example, although earlier texts would not
show it because they usually do not show this kind of emphasis:
compare 'I *do* love you' with 'I *love* you' and 'I *am* yours'. The
modern use of 'do' to stand in the position of the verb in these
four constructions (and to take its place entirely, as in 'You do,
don't you?') can be found in the sixteenth century and before,
but it is not an obligatory feature of literary English before 1700;
even thereafter the older use survived, especially in fixed phrases
like 'I know not'.

The pronoun 'thou', with its associated verb-ending (and its
plural, 'ye') also continued in use for some time after 1600, as did
the verb-ending '-eth' (instead of '-s') after 'he'. Shakespeare uses
both the older and the newer forms in both cases, sometimes (as
when Hamlet addresses his mother as 'you', and she calls him
'thou') with apparent nuances of difference; in these instances,
the nuance is no longer available within the grammar of English.

We have noticed that the unity of literary English is characterized by its availability to a diverse reading public, and we said
that the diversity was most striking if we took 'literary' widely,
to include newspapers and light novels. If we take it even more
widely, to include advertising (which we probably could if the
written word is our criterion for 'literary'), we may observe three
further developments in the English sentence, especially in the
verb, which are in a sense continuations of those which set the
1611 Bible apart from our present-day language. First of the three
is the 'unspeakable' sentence, the sort which belongs wholly to
the printed page: 'Tonight will be a gala occasion when such
stellar names as AB and CD will be joined by EF in a thrill-
packed extravaganza. . . .' A sub-type of the 'unspeakable'
sentence is one which could be spoken, but with a difference in
meaning. The sentence which reads 'Insist on . . . Buy a . . . Get
some . . .' is technically an imperative (it has no expressed subject

and no verb-ending), but in some kinds of writing it is not a command. Spoken, except when being read aloud, it remains a command; we should have to rephrase it if we wished to achieve the degree of enfeebled coaxing it has in print. The down-grading of the imperative is a feature of the literary language like the sentence which could not occur in speech.

The second type is similarly an unmarked verb that appears to be imperative, but here the force of the imperative mood is not even intended. It appears in newspaper headlines like 'Bombard Chungking' (in America; British newspapers would have 'Chungking Bombarded'). The American form is meant to have the force of the indicative mood, but the passive voice; that is, it gives the verb and its object, but no information about the subject. The British form accomplishes the same thing by using the passive voice. The American form represents a true develop-ment of the verb, because it is neither active nor passive in voice, neither indicative nor imperative in mood, but accomplishes an unambiguous meaning in certain contexts. It suggests a further reduction of word-endings of the sort we noticed throughout the period between the Conquest and 1700.

Another kind of reduction appears in the third development, although it is the opposite of the 'unspeakable' sentence. It is the sort that, until recently, was 'unprintable', not because it did not exist in speech, but because provision was not made for it within the rules of writing that differ from those of speech. I have in mind advertising phrases like 'Ever wonder how you've spent your . . .?' The phrase 'Did you . . . wonder' loses the position-marker 'do' and (as in the coaxing imperative and the voiceless, moodless verb) its subject; the phrase 'you have' contracts to an approximation of the form we employ in all speech but the most self-conscious.

Taken together, these three developments suggest that one effect of advertising and newspaper writing generally—which can ignore the extension in time demanded of other literary language, even if not the extension in space—has been to reorder the relationship between speech and writing. Writing retains and if anything increases its capacity to employ forms impossible or at least different in speech, but it accepts at the same time forms hitherto found in writing only when it was actually imitating or embodying speech (in the dialogue of a play or novel, for example). Since the time when Caxton first became aware of the impossibility of calling written speech 'literature', the distance between the primary form of language and its literary reflex has been kept by the conservative 'rules' of writing, and by the writers' awareness of these rules; any *rapprochement* was, by and large, an imposition of the writers' rules upon the habits of speech. With the changes that are typified by, but not restricted to, those in the verbal system I have just mentioned, writing shows in a large field of activity its capacity both to continue creating new possibilities from distinctively literary resources, and to incorporate some that are distinctively those of speech as well.

For Further Reading

C. Barber, *Linguistic Change in Present-Day English*, 1964.
B. Foster, *The Changing English Language*, 1968.
E. Partridge and J. W. Clark, *British and American English since 1900*, 1968.
S. Potter, *Changing English*, 1969.

II *The External History*

CHAPTER FIVE

The Middle Ages

Bede wrote his *Ecclesiastical History* in Latin. When he quoted the Old English poem on p. 4, he gave it in a Latin translation, adding 'this is the sense, not the order itself of the words; for poems, even though most excellently composed, cannot be translated literally from one language to another without detriment to their beauty and dignity'. Bede wrote in Latin, even though Old English of the Northumbrian dialect was his native language, for two main reasons. He meant his works for an international audience, and Latin was the language of international scholarship in his day, as for centuries before and after. And Latin had a stature amongst languages that gave it importance even in works like the *Ecclesiastical History* addressed primarily to one nation, even indeed when it meant translating a poem from the language of that very nation and losing the 'beauty and dignity' of the original. So although the almost universal use of Latin for serious writing in the West during much of the middle ages has its practical reasons, the reputation of the men who used it and of the works they wrote had another consequence. People wrote in Latin even when it was not necessary, so as to associate themselves with the authority and reputation of latinity. During most of this time all grammar books were grammars of Latin; books about literary style were in Latin and told how to write Latin; books on other subjects were in Latin too, and to read them the student had to learn Latin first. The Old English word

læden, 'Latin', came to mean *any* language because Latin was
the language.

When the eighth-century monastic culture in which Bede
flourished perished in the Viking raids, England lost touch with
the tradition of Latin learning. Towards the end of thé ninth
century King Alfred had thrown back the Vikings and was
ready to begin an educational programme that would restore
what had been lost. Alfred ordered a number of the most important books of Christian learning to be translated into English, so
that study could begin again with something the student knew—
his own language. This step, which seems so obvious to us, cost
Alfred much anxiety: was it proper to turn the fine old classics
into a language other than Latin? He reasoned that much Latin
learning was translated from the Greek, and some of the Greek
from the Hebrew, and justified himself with the historical
precedent. Alfred's programme had limited direct results, but its
influence is probably to be traced in the Old English translation
of Bede's *Ecclesiastical History*, and certainly in the fact that the
manifesto of the programme, Alfred's preface to the translation
of Gregory the Great's *Pastoral Care*, is one of the earliest documents in Old English that we have: almost all the Old English
manuscripts that survive come after it, and in greater or smaller
measure owe their existence to the programme that made the
native tongue a subject for study. Yet even this programme,
which gave England a thriving vernacular literature long before
most other European nations, was a virtue made of necessity.

Ælfric, who wrote the passage quoted on p. 5, lived about a
century after Alfred. He also wrote, amongst many other books,
a *Grammar*, *Glossary* and *Colloquy* for the teaching of Latin. In a
way his *Grammar* can be looked on as the next stage of Alfred's
educational reform: Ælfric translated and adapted two of the
best-known Latin grammars so that English students could use
their literacy in their own language to study Latin. Grammar,
he remarks, is the key to all learning, and his book may serve as
an introduction to both Latin and English grammar. It is a rare

thing for a medieval writer to notice any grammar but that of Latin, and Ælfric—who translated and paraphrased many Latin works—shows unusual interest and confidence in his native language. All the same, his confidence is incomplete: he remarks that many of the finer points of Latin literary diction can scarcely even be discussed in a language like Old English.

True, much Old English literature remains to us. But the Latin literature written in England during the same period is many times more extensive. It remains, in most cases, in many early manuscript copies, whereas Old English literature, especially the poetry, usually survives in only one copy. We know the names of most of the authors who wrote Latin literature in pre-Conquest England, and often we know a good deal about them besides the name. Old English literature, with a few exceptions amongst the prose, is virtually anonymous: we know here and there a name, but nothing about the man. And finally, the Latin literature that is distinctively English begins at the end of the seventh century; the Old English literature, although it may in some cases be older, survives, as we have seen, only in versions from the ninth and later centuries. All four points—the quantity of the books, the number of copies, their authorship, and their age—reflect the near domination of Latin as a literary medium in England before 1066.

After 1066, the picture changes. The Normans brought with them the Latin culture of the Continent, but they also brought with them their own vernacular, a dialect of French. Normans occupied high places in the government and Church, and so they controlled the schools in which literature was studied and written. Even three hundred years after the Conquest, the English-born king Edward III spoke French as his native language, and his Queen was French by birth; the leading court poet, Froissart, wrote in French. The continuation of French language and French influence at court does not mean that no English literature was being or had been written, but it suggests something of the slight interest which the centre of the aristocracy, in an age when an aristocratic patron meant much to a poet, had in English.

Already by 1180, an anonymous poet writing in the four-stress alliterating Old English verse form complained that the days of native teachers like Ælfric, who taught in English, were past: 'now it is the foreigners who teach our people'. (It is noteworthy that the manuscript collection in which the poem appears also contained Ælfric's Latin-English *Grammar* and *Glossary*.) Not until almost a hundred years later, towards 1300, does English for literary purposes reappear in any quantity. About that time Robert, a monk of Gloucester, wrote a vast history in verse. That he used verse at all for this purpose reflects the traditions of French historians, including Froissart a century later. (The *Old English Chronicle* was almost entirely in prose.) But that he wrote in English implies a returning confidence in the native vernacular for serious literature. He also tells us something about views of the language in his own day:

> The Normans could speak nothing but their own language,
> And spoke French as they did at home, and caused their
>   children to be taught the same,
> So that all high men of this land, that came of their blood,
> Keep to the same speech that they received from them;
> For unless a man knows French, men think little of him.
> But low men keep to English, and to their own speech still.
> I believe there are no countries in all the world
> That do not keep to their own speech, except England alone.
> But it is well known that it is good to know both.
>
> (*Chronicle*, 7538–7546)

The question of which language to speak or write, then, is both one of prestige and one of practicality. French was the language of the upper classes, and because class was largely a hereditary matter, the language reflected both the status and the lineage of the speaker. English remained the speech of the lower classes, the native peasantry. To be master of all situations and have the greatest social mobility, one needed to know both. The writer deplores a linguistic situation that heightens the differences between the classes and discredits the native language by barring it from influential use. We might guess that the division between upper-class French and lower-class English implies that only the French-speaking classes could read, for literacy was not widespread; but the very evidence of the poem contradicts our guess, for why would anyone write some 12,000 lines in a language no one could read? And the rapidly growing body of English works of the same time supports the same conclusion. From the late thirteenth century onwards more and more writers chose English, even though, like the monk of Gloucester, they employed French literary forms for the most part: histories, romances, dream allegories, lyrics, few of them in the native alliterating verse.

Of course Latin continued in use as well. About 1352 Ranulph Higden, a monk of Chester, wrote in Latin yet another vast history, which John of Trevisa translated into English thirty-three years later. The monk of Chester, like the monk of Gloucester, complained that English children were being forced to 'leave their own language, and to learn their lessons . . . in French, as they have since the Normans came first to England. Also gentlemen's children are taught to speak French from the time they are rocked in their cradles . . .; and rustic men wish to liken themselves to gentlemen, and seek with great eagerness to speak French, in order to be more respected'. When John came to translate the passage in 1385, he added a note that children in school now learned English instead of French, although he doubted the change was all for the good. Little by little, then, English was reasserting itself against Latin and French as the proper language for literature written in England. Edward III's French Queen died of the plague in 1369, and so did one Blanche, Duchess of Lancaster. Froissart, the court poet, wrote in French about the death of the Duchess, but it was the young court poet Chaucer, who, with his English *Book of the Duchess*, memorialized Blanche in what was to be the language of English literature ever after.

As we have seen, Chaucer's English reflects the period of

French domination even as it signals the end of that period, for his vocabulary in particular has much the same balance of native and French words as the language of our own day. So we find familiar such a dedication as that of Chaucer's *Troilus and Criseyde*, 'O moral Gower, this book I directe To the' (V.1856–7) (except in the treatment of final *-e*; we would write 'direct', 'thee'), and we assume that the reputation of the language, like its vocabulary, had reached the modern state of affairs by the late fourteenth century. The quotation from *Sir Gawain and the Green Knight* on p. 11 should remind us, however, how much such a judgement depends on the text we are studying: because Chaucer was so influential in forming our literary heritage, he seems familiar in terms of it. Here his mention of John Gower provides the contrasting illustration, for whilst Chaucer used French literary models but wrote in English, Gower wrote the first of his three major poems in French, the second in Latin, and only the third in English.

Near the beginning of his third book, Gower wrote

> . . . for that few men indite
> In our English, I shall make
> A book for England's sake.
> *(Confessio Amantis*, Prologue, 22–4)

Gower's first two huge works, and this remark in his third, all reflect his belief that the world of literature is the world of the Latin and French languages. John Lydgate, along with Chaucer and Gower the third great poet of the late middle ages in England, wrote mainly in English, but an English that paid homage to Latin and French by slavish imitation of their poetic diction (the 'aureate style'). He asks the subject of one poem

> Me to inspire of that I would indite
> With that balm, sent down by miracle
> When the Holy Ghost thee made his habitacle,
> And the liquor of thy grace shed
> Into my pen, t'enlumine this ditté,

Through thy support that I may proceed
Somewhat to say in laud and praise of thee.
(*Life of Our Lady*, I, 54–60)

From first to last during the middle ages, the status of English as a literary language was in doubt. The cultural reputation of Latin dwarfed it before the Norman Conquest, and the social prestige of French depressed it for centuries thereafter. Despite the example and influence of Chaucer's achievement, it was not until the Renaissance that the role of the English language in the literature of England was debated and settled.

For Further Reading

J. W. H. Atkins, *English Literary Criticism: The Medieval Phase*, 1952.
R. H. Robins, *Ancient and Mediaeval Grammatical Theory in Europe*, 1951.

CHAPTER SIX

The Renaissance

We have already seen that in the fifteenth and early sixteenth centuries Caxton (p. 17) and Skelton (p. 20) had, from their differing points of view, expressed concern about the English language. Caxton found it unstable; Skelton found it 'rude and rusty'. Caxton voiced his feelings in the prologue to a translation from the French; Skelton, in the poem quoted, solved his difficulty by turning to Latin for 'terms'. French and Latin had the qualities of elegance and stability that English seemed to lack, and translators in the early Renaissance often joined Caxton and Skelton in complaining that English could not do justice to the originals. But as we have already seen, Caxton's English and Skelton's had benefited greatly by the influx of words from French and Latin, and the influx continued in full spate during the rest of the sixteenth century.

It was exactly this influx that prompted yet another complaint against the state of the language in the early Renaissance. Readers who found strange words on every page of a new book soon came to resent them. In 1561 the Professor of Greek at Cambridge, Sir John Cheke, wrote

> Our own tongue should be written clean and pure, unmixed and unmangled with borrowing of other tongues, wherein if we take not heed by time, ever borrowing and never paying, she shall be fain to keep her house as bankrupt.
>
> (Letter to Thomas Hoby)

Cheke was doubtless thinking of the 'purity' of Greek itself—he tried to restore the pronunciation of Greek in his own day to the standard of the classical language—but his figures of speech suggest a different and deeper involvement: clean and pure on one hand, mixed and mangled on the other, the language is seen as a noble woman in danger of ruin and impoverishment. Linguistic borrowing or 'enrichment' becomes for Cheke a kind of wanton waste, threatening the integrity of a virtuous lady.

Most of the Renaissance debate about language in England avoided the real issues of linguistic interest—the process of linguistic change, the relationships of languages, the meaning of a linguistic standard, and so forth—and remained a matter of words about words: Skelton's 'rude and rusty' was Cheke's 'clean and pure', Skelton's 'polished terms' gave Cheke's 'mixed and mangled tongue'. Yet the debate was an active one, and Cheke's figure of speech about the bankrupt language had a remarkably long life: shortly before 1637 Ben Jonson, who had criticized Spenser's English, wrote

> Custom is the most certain mistress of language, as the public stamp makes the current money. But we must not be too frequent with the mint, every day coining.
>
> *(Timber)*

And in 1697, Daniel Defoe recommended the establishment of an authority that would make it 'as criminal . . . to coin words, as money' (*Essay upon Projects*).

In large measure, the debate had from the beginning a common ground of agreement: the English language was not fit to bear comparison with the learned languages of Europe, or to be employed for serious writing. This point of view, we can see, is carried over from much medieval thinking about English, although it is only in the Renaissance that the thinking comes out frequently in writing. The disagreement was about what steps were possible to remedy the deficiency. Some, like Skelton, turned instinctively to the languages whose reputation had always been high; some, like Cheke, felt that English needed to be strengthened from her own resources. Cheke himself attempted a translation of part of the Gospel of Matthew, in which he avoided as much as he could all borrowed words; yet his few real innovations in this cause, like 'mooned' for 'lunatic', are far outweighed by the many passages in which he accepted already traditional phrases of mixed vocabulary, like 'no man can serve two masters' (*Matt.* 6,24). 'Borrowed' words like 'serve' and 'master' had so long been part of the English vocabulary that even Cheke looked upon them as native.

At the opposite extreme the results were more vivid: it is easier to exaggerate a linguistic trend than it is to reverse it, and the 'nativists'—those of Cheke's opinion—had history against them. Those, on the other hand, who sought 'polished terms' to 'write ornately' soon found what they wanted. By the end of the century they had earned the name of 'inkhorn' writers, and the author of *The Art of Poesy* (1589, possibly George Puttenham) criticized the universities where such 'use much peevish affectation of words out of the primitive languages'. It was at much this time that Spenser published his *Faerie Queene*, and Shakespeare wrote his *Love's Labour's Lost*, where Holofernes, the Pedant, displays 'much peevish affectation':

> He draweth out the thread of his verbosity, finer than the staple of his argument. I abhor such fanatical phantasims, such insociable and point device companions, such rackers of orthography, as to speak dout fine, when he should say doubt; det, when he should pronounce debt; d e b t, not det: he clepeth a calf, cauf; half, hauf; neighbour *vocatur* nebour; neigh abbreviated ne: this is abhominable, which he would call abbominable. It insinuateth me of insanie: *ne intelligis domine*, to make frantic, lunatic.
>
> (V.i)

Holofernes typifies at least three late sixteenth-century attitudes towards English. First, of course, he is a glutton for ornate vocabulary. Second, he has a holier-than-thou view of others' language which leads him to make greater errors than the ones he criticizes (the pronunciations he objects to were probably common in educated circles, but 'abominable' does not come from *ab homine*), and so to misuse the very language he takes such pride in. And third, when faced with the gulf between the already long-established spelling and the ever-changing pronunciation, he stigmatizes the pronunciation. Shakespeare is exaggerating for purposes of satire, but the attitudes he satirizes were common. We have already remarked on the sources of the first two. The third, the renewed concern with the bearing of spelling on pronunciation, has a separate history.

By the middle of the sixteenth century, as we noted in chapter 3, spelling had become relatively fixed. It is only our own entirely rigid notion of spelling that makes any sixteenth-century forms seem at all odd. They were, compared with the current pronunciation, far out of date, and of course they made little attempt to mirror diversities of pronunciation. Whatever the reasons or advantages in such a situation, to someone like Cheke it was unsatisfactory. Cheke did not feel the need for a system like the modern International Phonetic Alphabet that provides a notation for the scientific study of language; such a study did not interest his century. And he probably had little idea of how the spellings of his day had come about. But to a man like him, who saw a benefit in restoring the ancient pronunciation of Greek, the reputability of a language, as well as its utility, came in part from the stability and accuracy of its spelling. Latin and Greek spellings were stable and accurate: they had been the subject of a number of special studies, including one by Bede. Cheke sought to bring to English a form of spelling that would put it on a par with the learned languages, and guard it from mispronunciation and even ridicule. In his proposed spelling, the passage quoted on p. 38 began 'our own tung shold be written cleane and pure, unmixt and unmangeled with borowing of other tunges, wherin if we take not heed by tijm. . . .'

Many writers joined the effort to 'save' English spelling.

Some, like Cheke, did no more than tailor the spelling to the pronunciation; others went further in proposing the use of special letters, or special typefaces, to indicate the individual sounds. Their systems, which have not survived, need not concern us greatly, but two scholars of the period have left interesting comments about the attempts. One was Richard Mulcaster, Spenser's teacher and Headmaster of the Merchant Taylors' School, who wrote 'they considered not, that . . . common reason and common custom . . . will never yield to any private conceit, which shall seem evidently either to force them or to cross them, as they themselves [the spelling reformers] do, never giving any precept, how to write right, till they have rated at custom, as a most pernicious enemy to truth and right, even in that thing, where custom hath most right, if it have right in any' (*Elementary*, 1582). And William Camden, Ben Jonson's teacher and Headmaster of Westminster School, wrote of the spelling reform 'which albeit sound and reason seem to countenance, yet that tyrant custom hath so confronted, that it will never be admitted' (*Remains*, 1605). Both men, speaking from positions of influence in literary circles, observed that the reform of spelling, however desirable and well devised, was impossible because 'custom', that is usage, had already become fixed.

The recognition of the role of usage in language was slow to come. Ben Jonson explained that by 'custom' (p. 39) he meant 'not the vulgar custom. . . . But that I call custom of speech, which is the consent of the learned.' The early Renaissance in England had, however, no registers of the consent of the learned about English, that is, no dictionaries or grammars, to act as linguistic reference books. For Latin there were many such books. Mulcaster called Latin 'exempt from custom . . . and laid up for knowledge' (*Positions*, 1581), that is, well-charted in dictionaries and grammars, and as a dead language no longer subject to changes brought about by usage. But the earliest dictionaries of English did little to 'lay it up for knowledge': in the sixteenth century, they were bilingual lists of words—French-English, Welsh-English, Spanish-English, Italian-English. They made scant attempt to record and analyse English in its own right. From the beginning of the seventeenth century, dictionaries of English alone began to appear, but they were all concerned with the 'hard words' of the language, the unfamiliar recent borrowings, technical and learned terms, and the like. None of them answered Mulcaster's demand years before for a work which 'would gather all the words which we use in our English tongue, whether natural or incorporate, out of all professions, as well learned as not, into one dictionary, and besides the right writing, which is incident to the alphabet, would open unto us therein both their natural force and their proper use'. Mulcaster here stipulated four requirements for the dictionary: it should contain all the words of the language, it should indicate their spellings, it should define their meanings, and it should regulate their use. No English dictionary of the Renaissance came near to fulfilling these requirements.

Nor were the grammars much better. While Latin grammars had long been a commonplace, grammars of English did not begin to appear until 1586, and then, as for long afterwards, they were little but attempts to describe the grammar of English in terms of the grammar of Latin: English was said to have a formally distinct ablative case, perfect infinitive, and so forth. From 1619 to the end of the seventeenth century some grammarians attempted to account more seriously for differences between Latin and English, but even so they either wrote in Latin, or had as their aim that 'our tongue may be made equal to those of the renowned countries, Italy and Greece' (Ben Jonson), so that a knowledge of Latin was necessary either to read the grammar, or to share in its assumptions. Little wonder that as late as 1693 the learned Dryden could complain 'we have yet . . . not so much as a tolerable dictionary, or a grammar, so that our language is in a manner barbarous' (*Discourse concerning Satire*). Dryden is using 'barbarous' in the old sense, 'not conforming to Latin and Greek standards of language', hence 'uncultured, unpolished'. Elsewhere he wrote

> I am often put to a stand, in considering whether what I write be the idiom of the tongue, or false grammar, and nonsense couched beneath that specious name of Anglicism; and have no other way to clear my doubts, but by translating my English into Latin, and thereby trying what sense the words will bear in a more stable language.
>
> (Dedication to *Troilus and Cressida*)

With no record of its vocabulary and structure in dictionaries and grammars, English had nowhere to set down the consent of the learned; and without their authority, it could not be regulated, polished and perfected.

Not every one in the Renaissance believed that the English language of his day was 'barbarous'. Mulcaster took 'this present period of our English tongue to be the very height thereof'. He wrote 'no one tongue is more fine than other naturally, but by industry of the speaker'; and 'I honour the Latin, but I worship the English'. And the great writers of the Renaissance in England, from Spenser and Shakespeare through to Milton, added to the confidence in English by their example and their achievement. Yet even Spenser toyed with the idea of adopting Latin and Greek metrical rules in English, and—as we have seen—employed his 'industry' to make English 'more fine'; while Milton first set about being a Latin poet. He did not write his poem 'Hail native language' until he was nineteen, and he continued to write poetry in Latin until he was almost fifty.

So the explicit Renaissance debate about the English language developed out of an implicit medieval view, heightened by the esteem in which the sixteenth and seventeenth centuries held Latin and Greek writers. In particular, the debate about the adequacy of English for literary composition questioned the comprehensiveness and elegance of the English vocabulary. It tried to open again the question of English spelling. It noticed the role of usage in language, but it was virtually without dictionaries and grammars to record usage, and quite without histories of the language to study its influence.

For Further Reading

R. F. Jones, *Triumph of the English Language*, 1953.
E. Vorlat, *Progress in English Grammar, 1585–1735*, 1964.
D. T. Starnes and G. E. Noyes, *The English Dictionary from Cawdrey to Johnson, 1604–1755*, 1946.
D. C. Douglas, *English Scholars*, 1939.

CHAPTER SEVEN

The Eighteenth Century

In 1816 a dictionary-maker could write, 'the English . . . have employed their talents successfully in every branch of literature, and in none more than that of philology' (George Crabb, *English Synonymes Explained*). Over a century before, Dryden (p. 43) had complained that the opposite was true. And halfway between them, in 1755, Dr Johnson wrote, 'I have devoted this book, the labour of years, to the honour of my country, that we may no longer yield the palm of philology, without a contest, to the nations of the Continent' (Preface to the *Dictionary*). The achievements of the eighteenth century which turned Dryden's pessimism to Crabb's optimism are typified by the toil and triumph of Dr Johnson.

The Renaissance debate over the English language continued in the eighteenth century, and many of the topics were the same: on the subject of vocabulary, for example, writers continued to question whether English words were not too few, or too harsh, or too intermingled with foreign borrowings, for elegant literature. But the debate, even though on the same topics, took a new shape: it was the century that saw the rise of the Royal Society (begun in 1662) and the incorporation of the Society of Antiquaries (1751); the *Commentaries* of Blackstone (1765) and the beginning of the *Encyclopædia Britannica* (1768); the assertion of parliamentary rule at home and the extension of the Empire in North America and the East. Such a century demanded order and regularity, and sought to gain them through the findings of science and the dictates of authority. In the study of the English language and the attitudes towards it, three movements stand out:

the plans for an English Academy, the making of the English dictionary, and the standardization of English grammar-books.

The idea of an English Academy to take as one of its duties the study and regulation of the English language had sources both abroad and at home. Abroad there were the academies of Italy and France. Their early foundation (1582 and 1635 respectively) and established activities, especially in compiling dictionaries, made them the envy of patriotic Englishmen. At home the Royal Society offered a basis on which to build such an Academy. For one thing, as a scientific body it was concerned to rid the language of any excesses or weaknesses of expression which would impede the communication of scientific discoveries. For another, it provided a forum for the most learned men of the day, whose rational and objective study of natural phenomena might well have included languages past and present, without the classical, patriotic or theological biases that had hampered earlier linguistic research. Finally, the desire to find a concise and accurate way of setting out scientific observations led a number of scientists to formulate artificial languages. In these there was a stable one-to-one relationship between the phenomenon and the word which described it, so that in Newton's notation *tor* referred to temperature; the prefix *u-* meant indefinitely in the positive extreme, *i-* in the negative, and *e-* midway between them. Hence *utor* meant 'hot', *itor* 'cold', *etor* 'tepid'. Such systems could be extended to any number of categories and states of being, and combined—as they were in some versions—with a kind of phonetic shorthand, they gave a constant relationship between the thing, the word, and the written symbol. But like any invented language, they could not circumvent the difficulties of natural language, because natural language was needed to explain their conventions, and because the categories of language are not the categories of nature.

In fact the Royal Society did attempt to perform some of the tasks of linguistic regulation. Soon after its foundation, John Dryden wrote 'I am sorry, that (speaking so noble a language as we do) we have not a more certain measure of it, as they have in France, where they have an Academy erected for that purpose' (Dedication to *The Rival Ladies*). Within a few months Dryden was among those the Royal Society appointed to a committee 'for improving the English language'. But the committee, which proposed such projects as the compilation of a grammar and a dictionary, did not flourish, and Dryden was still 'sorry' about the lack of a 'measure' when he wrote in 1693. And, as we have seen, Defoe, too (p. 39) proposed the establishment of an academy to act as the nation's linguistic authority.

To these notable literary advocates was added, in 1712, Jonathan Swift. By 1711 he had been discussing the state of the English language with Addison, who wrote about questions of language that 'will never be decided till we have something like an Academy, that by the best authorities and rules drawn from the analogy of languages shall settle all controversies between grammar and idiom' (*Spectator*, 135). In 1712 Swift published the first pamphlet that he allowed to go out under his own name, 'A Proposal for Correcting, Improving and Ascertaining the English Tongue'. Swift made a basic assumption for his plea:

> that our language is extremely imperfect; that its daily im-
> provements are by no means in proportion to its daily cor-
> ruptions; that the pretenders to polish and refine it, have chiefly
> multiplied abuses and absurdities; and, that in many instances,
> it offends against every part of grammar.

To remedy the situation, he recommended that there be appointed a group who

> will have the example of the French before them. . . . Beside
> the grammar-part, wherein we are allowed to be very defec-
> tive, they will observe many gross improprieties, which how-
> ever authorized by practice, and grown familiar, ought to be
> discarded.

Swift's notions and Addison's are very similar. Both speak of the perplexities and errors of 'the best writers'; both look to an

Academy for regulation in grammar and the use of words; and both thereby accept that usage ('idiom', 'practice') and grammar are divergent and even conflicting. Even 'the consent of the learned' will not lend weight to usage, for what else are 'the best writers' whose blunders they both condemn? Such condemnation implies an absolute standard, something revealed in the 'analogy of languages' approximating to Dryden's 'measure', of which the authority is greater than any usage, however sanctioned by long and widespread popular habit or literary employment.

But Swift did not propose only the 'correcting' and 'improving' of English; he sought also its 'ascertaining', that is, its 'fixing', so that it would never change again. For change, to Swift, was in language usually from better to worse; it closed the writings of one age to the readers of the next; and it was avoidable. When, forty-three years later, Dr Johnson called the 'Proposal' a 'petty treatise', he had in mind its hope of halting

> causes of change, which, though slow in their operation, and invisible in their progress, are perhaps as much superior to human resistance, as the revolutions of the sky, or intumescence of the tide,

and he noted

> With this hope, however, academies have been instituted, to guard the avenues of their languages, to retain fugitives, and repulse intruders; but their vigilance and activity have hitherto been vain; sounds are too volatile and subtle for legal restraints; to enchain syllables, and to lash the wind, are equally the undertakings of pride, unwilling to measure its desires by its strength.
>
> (Preface to the *Dictionary*)

Dr Johnson's criticism of Swift's 'Proposal' was not the first, but it summed up the arguments against it which, along perhaps with the political misfortunes of Swift's intended patron, caused it to fail. The agitation, especially among literary men, for an

English Academy for the regulation of the language, reached its climax and its end in Swift.

When, in 1754, Lord Chesterfield wrote

> I had long lamented that we had no lawful standard of our language set up, for those to repair to, who might choose to speak and write it grammatically and correctly: and I have as long wished that either some one person of distinguished abilities would undertake the work singly, or that a certain number of gentlemen would form themselves, or be formed by the government, into a society for that purpose,
>
> (Letter to *The World*)

he restated the need which had motivated Dryden, Defoe, Addison, and Swift, and he mentioned the obvious alternative to the idea of an academy: that a single scholar should compile a register of the language. He did so in an article recommending Dr Johnson's dictionary; and, as we have seen, it was in the Preface to the same dictionary that Dr Johnson had recognized his own work as a more suitable way than Swift's academy to win 'the palm of philology' from France and Italy.

The foreign-language dictionaries of the sixteenth century and the hard-word dictionaries of the seventeenth did little to answer Mulcaster's plea for a dictionary to compare with those of the Continent (p. 43). The mood of the eighteenth century, however, increasingly encouraged such a project. There were about fifteen dictionaries of English published between 1700 and 1755, not counting the many separate editions of some of the more popular ones, or Johnson's own. So when Johnson accepted a publisher's commission to write a dictionary in 1747, he was associating his own established literary reputation with a demonstrated linguistic interest of his age.

It took him eight years to produce the two large volumes that were published in 1755. The result far excelled anything that had appeared before, even in that century of dictionary activity. Johnson's dictionary begins with a lengthy Preface, setting out his views of the tasks of a dictionary-maker. It also contains a collection of examples of the language, arranged chronologically for the study of its history, and a short grammar. Johnson is the first English dictionary-maker to look upon his work as an aspect of the science of language: he provides, in addition to the dictionary proper, a theoretical statement, a historical perspective, and a grammatical summary.

In the number of words he collected, Johnson went far beyond his predecessors, even though he omitted many technical terms they had included. But it was his treatment of the words that was outstanding. A typical early eighteenth-century dictionary, like John Kersey's *General English Dictionary* (1708), attempts to list 'all sorts of difficult words', and leaves out common words like 'carry' except in their special uses in hawking and hunting. Nathaniel Bailey's *Dictionarium Britannicum* (1730), on which Johnson relied for some of his material, defines the transitive meaning of 'carry' simply as 'to bear or remove'; he borrows Kersey's definitions of the intransitive uses in hawking and hunting, and adds three others from navigation and horsemanship. He also notes that the word came from the French *charier*. Johnson adopts Bailey's etymology, and adds that the French word comes from Latin *currus*. He similarly borrows Bailey's definitions of the intransitive uses of 'carry' in hunting and horsemanship, but omits the uses in hawking and navigation as too technical. But where Kersey is silent on the more common meanings of the word, and Bailey gives only a vague paraphrase, Johnson sets out thirty-three distinct meanings in as many numbered paragraphs, illustrating each meaning with a group of quotations from the end of the sixteenth century to his own day: his first definition is illustrated by Dryden, Prior, Arbuthnot, and the King James Bible. The comprehensiveness of Johnson's dictionary, then, lay not only in its wordlist, although that was itself a great improvement over what went before. It lay rather in the meticulous specification of shades of meaning, and the illustration of these by carefully chosen quotations from noted authors. In the illustrations Johnson reintroduced the standard of the 'consent of the learned' into linguistic judgement, a standard which his own appointment as editor had already implied.

Some of Johnson's etymologies are wrong; he leaves out some important words, like 'descriptive', and includes others which are hardly English, like 'dubiosity'; some of his definitions are astray, and some are more playful than helpful; and his hope of suggesting standards for pronunciation and spelling was sometimes not realized. But even today a reader can make daily use of the book for a lifetime without being aware of any shortcomings. Its achievement in collecting and categorizing the vocabulary of English within an overall view of the nature of language was monumental. That it was the achievement of a man of letters, who drew on other men of letters as his authorities, gave the work particular influence in the formation of attitudes toward literary English.

The grammatical summary which Dr Johnson prefixed to his dictionary was, in large measure, a translation from the Latin of John Wallis' *Grammatica Linguae Anglicanae* (1653). It is striking that Johnson should have turned to a century-old book for his source, and even more striking that he added, 'I have collected rules and examples, by which the English language may be learned, if the reader be already acquainted with grammatical terms. ... To have written a grammar for such as are not yet initiated in the schools, would have been tedious, and perhaps at last ineffectual'. In an age when many grammars were being written, Johnson thought there had been no progress over the previous hundred years; in a book which treated the vocabulary comprehensively, Johnson despaired of a comprehensive approach to grammar.

Although Johnson's source was in Latin, its author recognized the mistake of grammarians who 'have forced our tongue too much into the pattern of Latin ... and so have taught many useless things about the cases of nouns, genders and declensions, and about the tenses, moods, and conjugations of verbs, about the government of nouns and verbs, etc., matters absolutely foreign to our language, producing confusion and obscurity rather than serving as explanations'. Yet Wallis sought to bring to his English grammar one feature of Latin grammar, namely the certainty and consistency of a dead literary language. Latin was, as Mulcaster had put it, 'exempt from custom and laid up for knowledge'. English, a living and therefore a changing language, various in various places then as now, could not be described in terms of such certainty. If the grammarian abandoned description for the imposition of 'rules', as many did, he not only ventured even further from the fact of linguistic variation over time and space; he also failed to apply to his own study Dr Johnson's notion of himself as one of those 'who do not form, but register the language; who do not teach men how they should think, but relate how they have hitherto expressed their thoughts'.

It was not enough, then, that grammarians should stop writing their books in Latin, or on Latin models. Dr Johnson's remarks reflect the inadequacy of the grammars of his own day. Along with the success of his dictionary, this inadequacy gave rise to a new generation of grammars, notably those of Robert Lowth and Lindley Murray. Lowth, a Hebrew scholar and divine who was later Bishop of London, brought out his book in 1762, for the purpose of answering Swift's complaint that the best authors 'offend against every part of grammar' (p. 48) which he quotes and agrees with. Lowth, then, will argue from absolute and unchangeable logic against any imagined 'offence', even if it has 'the consent of the learned'. In this view he is pre-Johnsonian.

Johnson, in his grammar, had said he would 'follow the common grammarians, without enquiring whether a fitter distribution might not be found'. Lowth defines (in terms which will be very familiar to most of us, largely because of Lowth's popularity and influence), the 'parts of grammar' he was thinking of. He calls the noun 'the name of any thing conceived to subsist, or of which we have any notion'. A preposition is 'put before nouns

and pronouns chiefly, to connect them with other words, and to
show their relation to those words'. Murray adopts both definitions, adding to the latter one, 'a preposition may be known by
its admitting after it a personal pronoun, in the objective case'.
But the Lowth–Murray definitions of both parts of speech will
also serve to define verbs. We say 'I like to come and go', 'I
dislike your comings and goings': 'come and go' refer to the
same thing as do 'comings and goings', yet only the latter are
nouns. Moreover, 'John married her' expresses the relation of
the pronoun 'her', which is in the objective case, to another
word, 'John'; yet 'married' is not a preposition. In short, these
are definitions that do not define. We *can* tell that 'come, go,
married' are not nouns or prepositions, but not in terms of the
definitions we are offered.

To be fair, both Lowth and Murray do realize that another
kind of description is possible. Lowth says 'a word which has the
article before it, and the possessive preposition *of* after it, must be
a noun. That participial words are sometimes real nouns is
undeniable; for they have a plural number as such: as "the
outgoings of the morning".' And Murray says that a noun 'may . . .
be distinguished by its taking an article before it, or by its making
sense of itself: as, a *book*, the *sun*, an *apple*; *temperance, industry,
chastity*'. Both writers here accept that we can identify a part of
speech by the endings it will take, and by the places it will
stand in a sentence. Yet their books do not carry the system
out.

Both writers also follow Johnson in supplying copious
examples, but where Johnson gave them as authorities, Lowth
and Murray give them as deplorable deviations. Lowth notes
that 'adjectives are sometimes employed as adverbs; improperly,
and not agreeably to the genius of the English language'. He then
quotes examples of the 'error' from Shakespeare, Dryden,
Clarendon, Swift, Addison, Pope, and the Bible . . . the same
sources Johnson drew on to lend authority to his work! If these
men can fail, how does Lowth come to know the 'genius of the

English language' by which they might have written better? The answer is that grammar, for him, is a set of 'rules' which exist outside the pattern of language itself.

Lowth is by no means, all the same, one of those who wish to force English into the shape of Latin. Commenting on an editor's alteration of the Miltonic 'he descending' (*Paradise Lost*, xii, 228) to 'him descending' on the analogy of the Latin ablative absolute, Lowth writes 'But *him* is not the ablative case, for the English knows no such case; nor does *him* without a preposition on any occasion answer to the Latin ablative. . . . This comes of forcing the English under the rules of a foreign language, with which it has little concern'. He is confident enough of the 'genius of the language' not to annex it to some supposedly superior tongue. But his confidence is misplaced: it is in the logic of absolute regulation rather than in the artifacts of language itself, even the King James Bible. The definitions and denunciations of Lowth and Murray have, we have seen, small relation to the realities of language, and already in their own day enough was known of these realities to contradict them. Yet their books went into endless editions, became the common quarry for later grammarians (even as Lowth was for Murray) and assumed, through their wide acceptance, the roles of eternal oracles: the fourth edition of a present-day grammar, dated 1952, says that a noun is 'the name of something' and a preposition 'a connecting word which shows the relation of a noun or pronoun to some other word in the sentence'. It is not easy to see why views which were already out of date in the authoritarian eighteenth century should have taken on the appearance of permanent validity, save perhaps that some people like to dictate, and some to be dictated to. It may be comforting to know you can avoid the 'errors' of Dryden, Swift, Pope, Addison, and the King James Bible, especially if you cannot write a masterpiece. Some of Dr Johnson's linguistic sympathy, if not his insight, may then stem from his literary powers. Be that as it may, the sympathy of one man was strengthened by the knowledge of many through a discovery of the late eighteenth century with which the nineteenth century completely altered the study of English.

For Further Reading

J. R. Hulbert, *Dictionaries British and American*, 1968.
S. A. Leonard, *The Doctrine of Correctness in English Usage, 1700–1800*, 1929.
I. Poldauf, *On the History of Some Problems of English Grammar before 1800*, 1954.
J. H. Sledd and G. J. Kolb, *Dr. Johnson's Dictionary*, 1955.
S. I. Tucker, *Protean Shape*, 1967.

CHAPTER EIGHT

The Modern Age

Swift and Dr Johnson were men of letters; Lowth, at one time Professor of Poetry in Oxford, was also an orientalist. His point of view is halfway between that of the man of letters as linguistic authority and the student of languages for their own sake. Another orientalist of the late eighteenth century, Sir William Jones, completes the series. Jones was a man of his age, the century of Blackstone's *Commentaries* and the extension of the Empire, for he was Chief Justice in Bengal. He was also a scholar and President of the Asiatic Society in Calcutta, to whom he communicated many of his findings. In 1786 he reported that the ancient language of India, Sanskrit, bore to Greek and Latin

> a stronger affinity, both in the roots of verbs and in the forms of grammar, than could possibly have been produced by accident; so strong indeed, that no philologer could examine them all three, without believing them to have sprung from some common source, which, perhaps, no longer exists: there is a similar reason, though not quite so forcible, for supposing that both the Gothic and the Celtic, though blended with a very different idiom, had the same origin with the Sanskrit.

Jones was not the first to trace the similarities between languages, but until his day the similarities had always been limited to single words: no one had seen them as part of a pattern, or as extending to 'the forms of grammar'. Those who did think of an original language usually assumed it still existed. Jones' hypothesis not only did away with this expectation. It implied a history of systematic linguistic change in which continuous differentiation of the original language stock produced a few great families of languages, and further divisions within these into languages, dialects, and so forth. This way of thinking about the known languages of the world is still accepted: the placing of Old English in European languages (p. 2) is an example of it.

Jones provided more than a 'model' of the history of Indian and European languages; he also helped teach Sanskrit to the West, and thereby to open to scholars a third pre-Christian language related to Greek and Latin. Where Greek has *eimí* for 'I am', Latin has *sum*. Sanskrit *ásmi* suggests a way in which the two are related. Similarly, for 'they are' Greek has *eisí*, Latin *sunt*, Sanskrit *sánti*. We can now see that the relationship goes beyond just one set of words, and can be roughly generalized as Greek *ei* = Latin *u* = Sanskrit *á*.

Before long, this 'comparative method' enabled other students to draw further conclusions. Observing that Latin *pater* was Old English *fæder*, Latin *caput* Old English *heafod*, Latin *centum* Old English *hundred*, and so on, they concluded the generalization Latin *c* = Old English *h*, Latin *t* = Old English *d*, Latin *p* = Old English *f*. These conclusions, with their extensions and modifications, defined a fixed relationship of similarity and difference between Germanic consonants (represented by Old English) and Indo-European consonants (represented by Latin). They were formulated by the Dane Rasmus Rask in 1814 and the German Franz Bopp in 1816; the improvements by Jacob Grimm in 1822 and Carl Verner in 1876 have given the formulations the names 'Grimm's law' and 'Verner's law'. But it was Rask, only twenty-six years after Jones gave his paper in Calcutta, who began the great era of linguistic study based on Jones' 'model' which has revealed most of what we now know about the history of human language.

The 'family tree' of languages revealed in this manner has three important characteristics. It deals only with related languages—roughly, Latin (and the languages descended from it, like French, Italian, Spanish, Portuguese), Greek, Celtic (like

Breton, Irish, Welsh), German (like German, Danish, Dutch, English), Slavonic (like Russian, Czech, Yugoslavian), Iranian, Armenian, Albanian, and Indian (like Sanskrit, Hindi). It looks on these languages in comparison with each other, and it traces the comparison historically. Given the nature of Jones' first insight, the historical-comparative approach to related languages is not hard to explain. But the three features have their limitations. The study of related languages provides no direct access to the understanding of languages which are unrelated, like Basque and Hungarian in Europe, or the tribal languages of Africa or America, or Chinese or Arabic. Historical-comparative formulations tell us little about the way most speakers of present-day languages, who have no knowledge of related tongues and their history, use their linguistic systems. Some beginnings of an approach to the systems of present-day languages in their own right can be seen in Lowth's remarks about the English participial nouns (p. 54); he identifies them in ways any English speaker would recognize, without reference to their place in a language family tree, or to the structure of another language.

The dramatic progress of the historical-comparative approach during the nineteenth century overshadowed the alternative approach, although some—notably missionaries and colonial administrators—were coming to terms with languages quite unlike the Indo-European ones. In the early twentieth century, however, men like Ferdinand de Saussure in Europe and Leonard Bloomfield in America were, in their different ways, concerned with approaches that did not depend on historical comparison of related and more or less familiar tongues. They were obliged to discover what features were common to all languages, and what were individual to a particular language. They soon found that many categories of grammar like 'noun' and 'verb', although so widespread in familiar languages that they seemed to be universal, were by no means shared by the unfamiliar languages they came to know.

Instead of concentrating on a 'parts of speech' approach, and deprived of the help of historical-comparative method, they discerned that all languages use a system of signals, and that the basic feature in the system was a contrast between 'same' and 'different'. Naturally they found a bewildering array of differences in the contrast between, say, 'elephant' and 'rhinoceros'. Both refer to pachyderms, but the similarity here is in nature, not in language.

The difference between 'night' and 'knight' is likewise in nature, and—by historical accident—in spelling. A more revealing contrast is between 'pig' and 'fig', 'peg', 'pit'. Of course the objects refer to differing things in nature, and indeed the last two could be verbs instead of nouns. But even without reference to the natural entities involved, or to the parts of speech, an English speaker hearing the words in isolated pairs like 'pig : fig', 'pig : peg', 'pig : pit' would know that they differed. By choosing items that differ in only one feature at a time, the smallest units of contrast can be highlighted. Further pairs would reveal further contrasts, but not infinitely. The investigator arrives at a list of units which contrast each with all the others: in known languages the list ranges from about 25 such units to about 75, and English has about 40.

Naturally, there are a great many ways in which these contrasts of sound can be signalled, and no language uses them all. We can easily hear the difference between 'big : pig' or 'pig : pick', because the contrasts 'b : p' and 'g : ck' depend on a very common English speech-signal, a buzzing in the throat which you may notice if you say the words with your fingers in your ears. Although this buzzing occurs in most languages, it does not enter into the system of signals in some of them. Speakers of such languages find it difficult or impossible to hear the difference between 'big : pig' to which our familiarity with English has so attuned us.

So *some* system of contrasts of sound, at a level often represented by individual letters in conventional English spelling, is basic to every language; but the total number of such contrasts varies,

as does the employment of distinctive features like the buzzing
in the throat. Such contrasts can be built up into larger units,
like 'pig'. We have no word 'pi' or 'ig', but we have 'pigs',
which contains 'pig' and 's'. 'Pig' therefore contains no meaningful unit smaller than itself but larger than 'p', 'i' and 'g'; 'pigs'
contains two units smaller than itself. The second unit, which we
spell 's' but pronounce 'z', cannot stand by itself, but it has a
certain meaning which 'p', 'i' and 'g' have not. If we concentrate
on the sound, we shall notice that this meaningful 's' has three
pronunciations, as in 'pigs', 'cats', 'horses': it sounds like 'z', 's'
and 'iz'. All three creatures are domestic mammalian quadrupeds,
so the change in pronunciation has nothing to do with the
natural status. It has merely to do with the sound before 's':
after vowels (as in 'fleas') and consonants which, like 'g', are
made with the buzzing in the throat, it appears as 'z'; after
consonants made without buzzing, as 's'; after 's', 'z', 'sh', 'ch',
as 'iz'. The changes do not alter the meaning, which is roughly
'plural'. Of course the unit of meaning, 's plural', is made up of
units from the list of sound-contrasts in English, just as is 'pig':
but 's plural' is made up of only one such unit, while 'pig' is
made up of three.

If we were learning English simply by observing the speech of
an English speaker, we should at this point be able to say that
there is a list of about 40 mutually contrasting sounds in the
language, each of which is part of a signal but has no meaning in
itself. Units which do have meaning are made up of one or more
items from this list. Some meaningful units can stand alone, and
some appear only when attached to others: consider 'pig-ish-
ness'. In short, the language is made up of units from the smallest
to the larger and the largest, according to certain 'rules': you
cannot say 'nessishpig', although the units are all good English,
and you cannot pronounce 'pigs' with the same 's' as in 'cats'.
As Lowth perceived, it is the behaviour in accordance with
other rules—the addition of 's plural' to 'outgoing', for example,
and the possibility of putting 'the' before it—that most helpfully

identifies 'outgoings' as a noun, for we cannot say 'the to go out' or 'to go outs'.

Carried through the whole language, such a method reveals its 'structure'—a term that recalls the building of houses (here, sentences) from small units like bricks (which may be made up of varying ingredients, but are bricks just the same) to walls and ceilings, rooms, and so forth (here, phrases and clauses). Obviously such an approach is helpful in English, but it also corresponds to patterns common to all known human languages, without making irrelevant comparisons between them, or depending on their history or familiarity.

The structural view, which describes a language at one point in time and in its own right, clearly differs greatly from the historical-comparative view. In fact, both approaches have much to offer the student of language, and each has learned much from the other. But the structural view is not the only one which describes a language in its own terms at a single point in time. Few of us feel that we are behaving according to this view of language when we speak, any more than we feel we are employing a collateral descendant of Latin *pater* when we say 'father'. We would not need, for example, a structural insight in order to solve the following problem:

The cat sees the bird : The bird is seen by the cat.
John loves Mary :   ?

We should volunteer 'Mary is loved by John', although it is an ugly, awkward sentence, and—consequently—one we have probably never heard before, no matter how many couples we know by those names. There is a pattern of relationships amongst the possible sentences of English that enables us to bring forth 'Mary is loved by John', if we wish to, on the basis of our experience of the language, even if we have never heard the sentence before. Similarly the questions would be 'Does John love Mary?', and 'Is Mary loved by John?'. We supply 'does' in the first sentence but change the position of 'is' in the second, as we observed on p. 27.

Not only have these corresponding sentences fixed relationships; they have a fixed order. We should be confused if, in learning English, we first encountered 'Does John love Mary?' or 'Mary is loved by John' or 'Is Mary loved by John?'. It is easier and more natural to think of 'John loves Mary' as the basic sentence, 'Mary is loved by John' as an alteration of it, and 'Is Mary loved by John?' as an alteration of *that*. Similarly, it is easiest to arrive at 'Does John love Mary?' direct from 'John loves Mary' instead of by way of 'Is Mary loved by John?'. What is more, the rules for the alterations can be most concisely stated if we go about things in this way. As we saw on p. 27, such rules are so concise that they will account in a short formula for the use of 'do' in a wide number of cases.

This approach, which transforms one sentence into another, sees the end product as having been 'generated' according to such rules. The rules, which are general and therefore abstract, come first; the sentence comes last. The generative system describes language by analysing the steps from the abstraction to the particular sentence, and as we have seen, it tells us much about the way the language—English or another, in which different rules would apply—really works. The structural system, on the other hand, given a particular sentence, works back the other way towards the abstraction, down to dividing 'pigs' into 'pig' and 's' with the labels 'noun' and 's plural' and so forth. The two approaches work in different directions and achieve different ends, but both have their place in helping us to understand our language just as the historical-comparative view likewise continues to have. It is a question of the right tool for the job, the suitable means for an end.

As we have noticed at the beginning of the chapter, these three approaches all have their roots in a historical situation, one in which the man of letters was playing a decreasing role in the study of language. To some extent, it is true, literature and linguistics became separated in the nineteenth century and remain so today: literature is 'art', and the study of language has turned into a 'science'. But the separation is neither total nor desirable, nor even necessary. Some men of letters have continued to interest themselves in the fruits of linguistic research. As early as 1829, the English essayist William Hazlitt protested that the findings of philology offered a better basis for teaching English grammar than did the rules of Greek and Latin 'applied . . . indiscrimately and dogmatically' to English, and he pointed out that the 38th edition of Murray's grammar perpetuated false notions long since disproved (*The Atlas*, 15 March).

At the turn of the century George Bernard Shaw called for a reform of spelling, so that a student would be taught 'by instruction in the phonetic alphabet, and by having a standard pronunciation suggested to him on every printed page' (*Morning Leader*, 16 August 1901). The idea that phonetic spelling would, by its very accuracy, promote standard pronunciation is an old one—it was put forward by Noah Webster for the creation of a distinctive American way of speech a century before Shaw, and the distinctive speech, without the spelling, developed all the same. But Shaw's interest was excited by other kinds of political views: 'the question of the nationalisation of the existing class monopoly of orthodox English speech'. He was also inspired by the recent development in the historical study of sounds, and in particular by the establishment of a senior academic post in such studies at Oxford. His hope that pronunciation would accord itself to phonetic spelling is a false one, as a closer study of the history of the language would have shown him, and Dr Johnson knew better than to hope that spelling according to pronunciation would retain its accuracy long. Shaw was, like some other men of letters, stimulated by the study of language without really becoming fully expert in it.

The same might be said of the founders of the Society for Pure English, especially Robert Bridges, who became Poet Laureate the year the Society began, 1913. In a statement of motives in 1919, he wrote:

In certain respects the English language is in its present condition inferior to some of its rivals as a convenient carrier of thought; and it would be a disgrace to us if we made no effort to bring it up to the mark. . . . Now the history of languages shows that there is danger lest our speech should grow out of touch with our literature, and losing, as it were, its capital, and living from hand to mouth, fall from its nobility and gradually dissociate itself from apparent continuity with its great legacy.

(Tract, XXI)

Bridges' remarks recall Cheke's and Swift's, particularly in the figurative terms he uses: languages for him are rivals, men suffer disgrace who do not help to improve them, language which does not keep its budget will itself 'fall from nobility'. Bridges has good words to say about the great *Oxford English Dictionary on Historical Principles* which began in the late nineteenth century and had almost completed publication in his day, and some of his colleagues in the Society for Pure English were distinguished students of language. But his figurative terms betray ideas that more serious acquaintance with the study of language would certainly have corrected: rivalry is not part of the history of languages, men have little influence in directing linguistic change, there is no such thing as a 'mark' up to which language can be brought, the history of languages says nothing about danger, and above all language is in no way comparable to a spendthrift nobleman.

In our own day, although language plays its part in some University departments of English where many receive their training who will teach in school, and although the novelist Anthony Burgess has written a well-informed book about language, the gulf between language and literary studies that began to open at the beginning of the nineteenth century remains wide and is perhaps widening. Three reasons at least suggest themselves for bridging the gap:

1. Students of English, whether or not they teach, will be

looked on as arbiters on matters of language by those around them. They have a duty to be well-informed.

2. Although Shaw's 'nationalisation of orthodox English' was a will-of-the-wisp, language still has an exaggerated place in social distinctions. A rational attitude toward usage, dialects, and linguistic change will do much to put such distinctions into perspective.

3. The medium of literature is language. As we saw on p. 24, the student who does not know something of the history of his tongue cannot read any but the most recent works accurately. Moreover, knowledge of the structure of the language is indispensable to the understanding of literary style of all periods.

These reasons stem from the utility of linguistic study, the aid it can give to other studies and activities. But in addition we should recall that one Old English compound for 'man' was *reordberend*, 'speech-bearer', recognizing that speech is uniquely a human attribute. It reminds us that the study of such an attribute for its own sake will always be humane.

For Further Reading

A. Arlotto, *Introduction to Historical Linguistics*, 1971.
T. E. Berry, *The Study of Language*, 1971.
L. Bloomfield, *Language*, 1933.
F. Brengelman, *The English Language*, 1970.
A. Burgess, *Language Made Plain*, 1969.
D. Crystal, *What is Linguistics?*, 1968.
A. E. Darbyshire, *A Description of English*, 1967.
F. P. Dinneen, *An Introduction to General Linguistics*, 1967.
W. N. Francis, *The Structure of American English*, 1958.
W. N. Francis, *The English Language*, 1970.
J. P. Friend, *An Introduction to English Linguistics*, 1967.
C. C. Fries, *The Structure of English*, 1952.
H. A. Gleason, Jr., *Linguistics and English Grammar*, 1965.
A. A. Hill, *Introduction to Linguistic Structures*, 1958.
C. F. Hockett, *A Course in Modern Linguistics*, 1958.
O. Jespersen, *Essentials of English Grammar*, 1933.
J. R. Keller, *Linguistic Theory and the Study of English*, 1968.
R. W. Langacker, *Language and its Structure*, 1968.

R. Lass, *Approaches to English Historical Linguistics*, 1969.
W. P. Lehmann, *Historical Linguistics*, 1962.
R. B. Long, *The Sentence and its Parts*, 1961.
A. H. Marckwardt, *Introduction to the English Language*, 1942.
A. H. Marckwardt, *American English*, 1958.
J. C. McLaughlin, *Aspects of the History of English*, 1970.
E. Partridge, *The World of Words*, 1950.
S. Potter, *Modern Linguistics*, 1957.
R. Quirk, *The Use of English*, 1962.
R. H. Robins, *General Linguistics*, 1964.
E. Sapir, *Language*, 1963.
F. de Saussure, *Course in General Linguistics*, 1959.
N. C. Stageberg, *An Introductory English Grammar*, 1971.
B. M. H. Strang, *Modern English Structure*, 1968.
E. H. Sturtevant, *An Introduction to Linguistic Science*, 1960.
J. T. Waterman, *Perspectives in Linguistics*, 1963.

HISTORY OF LINGUISTIC AND ENGLISH STUDIES:

J. B. Carroll, *The Study of Language*, 1953.
D. J. Palmer, *The Rise of English Studies*, 1965.
H. Pedersen, *The Discovery of Language*, 1962.
R. H. Robins, *A Short History of Linguistics*, 1967.

THE ROLE OF LINGUISTICS IN LITERARY CRITICISM:

S. Chatman, *Literary Style*, 1971.
D. Crystal and D. Davy, *Investigating English Style*, 1969.
A. E. Darbyshire, *A Grammar of Style*, 1971.
G. Devoto, *Linguistics and Literary Criticism*, 1963.
R. Fowler, *Essays on Style and Language*, 1966.
R. Fowler, *The Languages of Literature*, 1971.
D. C. Freeman, *Linguistics and Literary Style*, 1970.
T. A. Sebeok, *Style in Language*, 1960.
J. Spencer, *Linguistics and Style*, 1965.
V. Tufte and G. Stewart, *Grammar as Style*, 1971.
S. Ullmann, *Language and Style*, 1964.

TRANSFORMATIONAL-GENERATIVE GRAMMAR

E. Bach, *An Introduction to Transformational Grammars*, 1964.
R. Fowler, *An Introduction to Transformational Syntax*, 1971.
R. D. King, *Historical Linguistics and Generative Grammar*, 1969.
M. Lester, *Introductory Transformational Grammar of English*, 1971.
B. L. Liles, *Introductory Transformational Grammar*, 1971.

Translations of Matthew 6, 24–34

Students of the English language often compare versions of a single text made in different centuries, to discover or demonstrate in concrete terms something of the changes that took place. William Camden, perhaps the first to do so, chose the *Lord's Prayer* for his example, because the Bible is the only text of which a new version is available in each stage of the history of English from the oldest to the most recent. For this purpose the Bible has the same drawback as the *Ancrene Wisse* (see p. 9): religious texts are almost always conservative in their diction. Earlier translations of the Bible, moreover, frequently have a heavy influence on later ones. And translators of the New Testament go some to the Greek and some to the Latin versions; even those translating from the same language have employed different editions with different readings.

Even so, comparison of such texts in chronological order can tell us much. The Bible has been the literary document *par excellence* in every age of English literature, and its successive versions both reflected and influenced literary taste and the state of the language. Literary taste is involved in changes of style; they are the outcome of a choice the author could make amongst several available ways of saying something. The state of the language, on the other hand, dictated which ways were available.

Old English, Tenth Century

Ne mæg nān man twām hlāfordum þēowian, oððe
hē sōþlīce ænne hataþ, and ōðerne lufaþ; oððe hē biþ
ānum gehȳrsum, and ōðrum ungehȳrsum. Ne magon
gē Gode þēowian and woruldwelan. Forðām ic secge
ēow, ðæt gē ne sīn ymbhȳdige ēowre sāwle, hwæt gē
eton; ne ēowrum līchaman, mid hwām gē sȳn ymb-
scrȳdde. Hū nys sēo sāwl sēlre ðonne mete, and ēower
līchama betera ðonne ðæt rēaf? Behealdaþ heofonan
fuglas, forðām ðe hig ne sāwaþ, ne hig ne rīpaþ, ne hig
ne gadriaþ on berne; and ēower heofonlīca fæder hig
fēt. Hū ne synt gē sēlran ðonne hig? Hwylc ēower
mæg sōþlīce geþencan ðæt hē ge-ēacnige āne elne tō hys
anlīcnesse? And tō hwī synt gē ymbhȳdige be rēafe?
Bescēawiaþ æcyres lilian, hū hig weaxaþ. Ne swincaþ
hig, ne hig ne spinnaþ; Ic secge ēow sōþlīce, ðæt furðon
Salomon on eallum hys wuldre næs oferwrigen swā
swā ān of ðyson. Sōþlīce gyf æcyres wēod, ðæt ðe tō-
dæg is, and biþ tō-morgen on ofen āsend, God scrȳt,
ēalā gē gehwædes gelēafan, ðām mycle mā hē scrȳt
ēow? Nellen gē eornustlīce bēon ymbhȳdige, ðus cweð-
ende, Hwæt ete wē? oððe, Hwæt drince wē? oððe,
Mid hwām bēo wē oferwrogene? Sōþlīce ealle ðās þing
þēoda sēceaþ; wıtodlīce ēower fæder wāt ðæt gē ealra
ðyssa þinga beþurfon. Eornustlīce sēceaþ ærest Godes
rīce and hys rihtwīsnesse, and ealle ðās þing ēow bēoþ
ðær-tō ge-ēacnode. Ne bēo gē nā hogiende ymb ðā
morgenlīcan nēode, sōþlīce se morgenlīca dæg caraþ
ymb hyne sylfne; æghwylc dæg hæfþ genōh on hys
āgenum ymbhogan.

John Wiclif (or a follower), about 1390

No man may serue to two lordis, forsothe ethir he shal haat the toon, and loue the tother; other he shal susteyn the toon, and dispise the tothir. ʒe mown nat serue to God and richessis. Therfore Y say to ʒou, that ʒe ben nat besie to ʒoure lijf, what ʒe shulen ete; othir to ʒoure body, with what ʒe shuln be clothid. Wher ʒoure lijf is nat more than mete, and the body more than clothe? Beholde ʒe the fleeʒinge foulis of the eir, for thei sowen nat, ne repyn, neither gadren in to bernys; and ʒoure fadir of heuen fedith hem. Wher ʒe ben nat more worthi than thei? Sothely who of ʒou thenkinge may putte to his stature oo cubite? And of clothing what ben ʒe besye? Beholde ʒe the lilies of the feelde, how thei wexen. Thei traueilen nat, nether spynnen; Trewly I say to ʒou, for whi neither Salamon in al his glorie was keuerid as oon of thes. For ʒif God clothith thus the heye of the feeld, that to day is, and to morwe is sente in to the fourneyse, how moche more ʒou of litil feith? Therfore nyl ʒe be bisie, sayinge, What shulen we ete? or, What shulen we drynke? or, With what thing shulen we be keuered? Forsothe heithen men sechen alle these thingis; trewly ʒoure fadir wote that ʒe han need to alle these thingis. Therfore seke ʒee first the kyngdam of God and his riʒtwisnesse, and alle these thingis shulen be cast to ʒou. Therfore nyle ʒe be besie in to the morwe, for the morew day shal be besie to it self; sothely it sufficith to the day his malice.

William Tyndale, 1525

No man can serve two masters. For other he shall hate the one, and love the other: or els he shall lene to the one, and despise the other. Ye can nott serve God and mammon. Therefore I saye vnto you, be not carefull for youre lyfe, what ye shall eate, or what ye shall dryncke, nor yet for youre boddy, what rayment ye shall weare. Ys not the lyfe, more worth then meate? and the boddy more off value then rayment? Beholde the foules of the aier: for they sowe not, neder reepe, nor yet cary into the barnes, and yett youre hevenly father fedeth them. Are ye not better then they? Whiche off you (though he toke thought therefore) coulde put one cubit vnto his stature? And why care ye then for rayment? Beholde the lyles off the felde, howe they growe. They labour not nether spynn, And yet for all that I saie vnto you that even Solomon in all his royalte, was nott arayed lyke vnto one of these. Wherfore yf God so clothe the grasse, which ys to daye in the felde and to morowe shalbe cast into the fournace: shall he not moche more do the same vnto you, o ye off lytle fayth? Therfore take no thought saynge: what shall we eate, or what shall we dryncke, or wherewith shall we be clothed (Aftre all these thynges seke the gentyls) for youre hevenly father knoweth that ye have neade off all these thynges. But rather seke ye fyrst the kyngdom off heven, and the rightewesnes ther of, and all these thynges shalbe ministred vnto you. Care not therfore for the daye foloynge. For the daye foloynge shall care ffor yt sylfe. Eche dayes trouble ys sufficient for the same silfe day.

Authorized (King James) Version, 1611

No man can serue two masters: for either he will hate the one and loue the other, or else hee will holde to the one, and despise the other. Ye cannot serue God and Mammon. Therfore I say vnto you, Take no thought for your life, what yee shall eate, or what ye shall drinke, nor yet for your body, what yee shall put on: Is not the life more then meate? and the body then raiment? Behold the foules of the aire: for they sow not, neither do they reape, nor gather into barnes, yet your heauenly father feedeth them. Are yee not much better then they? Which of you by taking thought, can adde one cubite vnto his stature? And why take ye thought for raiment? Consider the lilies of the field, how they grow: they toile not, neither doe they spinne. And yet I say vnto you, that euen Solomon in all his glory, was not arayed like one of these. Wherefore, if God so clothe the grasse of the field, which to day is, and to morrow is cast into the ouen: shall he not much more clothe you, O yee of little faith? Therefore take no thought, saying, What shall we eate? or, what shall we drinke? or wherewithall shall wee be clothed? (For after all these things doe the Gentiles seeke:) for your heauenly father knoweth that ye haue neede of all these things. But seeke ye first the kingdome of God, and his righteousnesse, and all these things shalbe added vnto yo . Take therefore no thought for the morrow: for the morrow shall take thought for the things of it selfe: sufficient vnto the day is the euill thereof.

John Wesley, 1755

No man can serve two masters: for either he will hate the one and love the other, or he will cleave to the one and neglect the other. Ye cannot serve God and Mammon. Therefore I say unto you, Take not thought for your life, what ye shall eat, nor for the body, what ye shall put on. Is not the life more than meat, and the body than raiment? Behold the birds of the air: they sow not, neither do they reap, nor gather into barns; yet your heavenly Father feedeth them. Are ye not much better than they? And which of you by taking thought can add to his age the smallest measure? And why take ye thought for raiment? Consider the lilies of the field, how they grow; they toil not, neither do they spin: And yet I say unto you, that even Solomon in all his glory was not arrayed like one of these. Now: if God so clothe the grass of the field, which to day is, and to morrow is cast into the still, will he not much more clothe you, O ye of little faith? Therefore take not thought, saying, What shall we eat, or what shall we drink, or what shall we wear? (For after all these things do the heathens seek) for your heavenly Father knoweth that ye need all these things. But seek ye first the kingdom of God and his righteousness, and all these things shall be added to you. Take not therefore thought for the morrow: for the morrow shall take thought for itself: sufficient for the day is the evil thereof.

Appendix A

Revised Version, 1881

No man can serve two masters: for either he will hate the one, and love the other; or else he will hold to one, and despise the other. Ye cannot serve God and mammon. Therefore I say unto you, Be not anxious for your life, what ye shall eat, or what ye shall drink; nor yet for your body, what ye shall put on. Is not the life more than the food, and the body than the raiment? Behold the birds of the heaven, that they sow not, neither do they reap, nor gather into barns; and your heavenly Father feedeth them. Are not ye of much more value than they? And which of you by being anxious can add one cubit unto his stature? And why are ye anxious concerning raiment? Consider the lilies of the field, how they grow; they toil not, neither do they spin: yet I say unto you, that even Solomon in all his glory was not arrayed like one of these. But if God doth so clothe the grass of the field, which to-day is, and to-morrow is cast into the oven, shall he not much more clothe you, O ye of little faith? Be not therefore anxious, saying, What shall we eat? or, What shall we drink? or, Wherewithal shall we be clothed? For after all these things do the Gentiles seek: for your heavenly Father knoweth that ye have need of all these things. But seek ye first his kingdom, and his righteousness; and all these things shall be added unto you. Be not therefore anxious for the morrow: for the morrow will be anxious for itself. Sufficient unto the day is the evil thereof.

Basic English, 1941

No man is able to be a servant to two masters: for he will have hate for the one and love for the other, or he will keep to one and have no respect for the other. You may not be servants of God and of wealth. So I say to you, Take no thought for your life, about food or drink, or about clothing for your body. Is not life more than food, and the body more than its clothing? See the birds of heaven; they do not put seeds in the earth, they do not get in grain, or put it in storehouses; and your Father in heaven gives them food. Are you not of much more value than they? And which of you by taking thought is able to make himself a foot taller? And why are you troubled about clothing? See the flowers of the field, how they come up; they do no work, they make no thread: But I say to you that even Solomon in all his glory was not clothed like one of these. But if God gives such clothing to the grass of the field which is here today, and tomorrow is put into the oven, will he not much more give you clothing, O you of little faith? Then do not be full of care, saying, What will we have for food or drink? or, With what may we be clothed? Because the Gentiles go in search of all these things: for your Father in heaven has knowledge that you have need of all these things: But let your first care be for his kingdom and his righteousness; and all these other things will be given to you in addition. Then have no care for tomorrow: tomorrow will take care of itself. Take the trouble of the day as it comes.

J. B. Phillips, 1952

No one can be loyal to two masters. He is bound to
hate one and love the other, or support one and despise
the other. You cannot serve God and the power of
money at the same time. That is why I say to you,
don't worry about living—wondering what you are
going to eat or drink, or what you are going to wear.
Surely life is more important than food, and the body
more important than the clothes you wear. Look at the
birds in the sky. They never sow nor reap nor store
away in barns, and yet your Heavenly Father feeds them.
Aren't you much more valuable to him than they are?
Can any of you, however much he worries, make himself an inch taller? And why do you worry about clothes?
Consider how the wild flowers grow. They neither
work nor weave, but I tell you that even Solomon in
all his glory was never arrayed like one of these! Now
if God so clothes the flowers of the field, which are
alive today and burnt in the stove tomorrow, is he not
much more likely to clothe you, you 'little-faiths'? So
don't worry and don't keep saying, 'What shall we eat,
what shall we drink or what shall we wear?'! That is
what pagans are always looking for; your Heavenly
Father knows that you need them all. Set your heart on
his kingdom and his goodness, and all these things will
come to you as a matter of course. Don't worry at all
then about tomorrow. Tomorrow can take care of
itself! One day's trouble is enough for one day.

New English Bible, 1961

No servant can be slave to two masters; for either he will hate the first and love the second, or he will be devoted to the first and think nothing of the second. You cannot serve God and Money. Therefore I bid you put away anxious thoughts about food and drink to keep you alive, and clothes to cover your body. Surely life is more than food, the body more than clothes. Look at the birds of the air; they do not sow and reap and store in barns, yet your heavenly Father feeds them. You are worth more than the birds! Is there a man of you who by anxious thought can add a foot to his height? And why be anxious about clothes? Consider how the lilies grow in the fields; they do not work, they do not spin; and yet, I tell you, even Solomon in all his splendour was not attired like one of these. But if that is how God clothes the grass in the fields, which is there today, and tomorrow is thrown on the stove, will he not all the more clothe you? How little faith you have! No, do not ask anxiously, 'What are we to eat? What are we to drink? What shall we wear?' All these are things for the heathen to run after, not for you, because your heavenly Father knows that you need them all. Set your mind on God's kingdom and his justice before everything else, and all the rest will come to you as well. So do not be anxious about tomorrow; tomorrow will look after itself. Each day has troubles enough of its own.

A Select Glossary of Linguistic Terms not Included in the Text

Ablaut. Same as **Gradation**.

Acronym. Word formed from initial letters (*UNESCO*) or syllables (*radar*) of words in a phrase.

Affix. A prefix, infix, or suffix.

Affricate. Stop with gradual release; the initial and final sounds in 'church', 'judge'.

Agglutinative. Syntactical system depending on combination of roots into compounds without change of form or meaning; basis of Turkish, Hungarian, etc.

Alveolar. Consonant articulated with the tongue near the alveolar ridge behind the upper front teeth; the initial and final sounds in 'dent', 'cheese', 'loan', 'shorts'.

Amelioration. Elevation of the semantic content of a word, as modern 'knight' from Old English *cniht*, 'youth, foot warrior'.

Analogy. Influence of general patterns of a language (e.g., 's plural') making individual items ('man') conform to the pattern (giving plural 'mans').

Analytic. Syntactical system depending on word-order, as Modern English differentiates between 'Dog bites man' and 'Man bites dog'.

Articulation. Production of speech sound; the movements of speech organs to produce it; the sound itself.

Aspirate. Consonant articulated ('h' in 'hall') or followed ('p' in 'pie', but not in 'spy') by a puff of air.

Assimilation. Change of a speech sound in conformity with another adjacent, as 'assimilate' from Latin *ad-similo*.

Back formation. Creation of mistakenly supposed original form from existing word through its derivative, as 'beg' from 'beggar'.

Blend. Word formed by combination of parts of two existing words, as 'motel', 'astronaut'.

Case. Categories signalled by inflexional forms of modern English nouns and pronouns, and in addition of Old English adjectives. Nouns now have two cases ('man, man's') and pronouns three ('he, him, his').

Clause. A linguistic structure containing a finite verb, which may stand alone (as a sentence) even though a single word: 'Stop!', or may stand in a sentence where a single word might also stand.

Closed syllable. One ending with a consonant, as both in 'tiptop'.

Close Vowel. One articulated with the tongue high in the mouth; the vowel sounds in 'he', 'who'.

Cognate. Word related to another by common descent, as French *père* to Spanish *padre* (from Latin *pater*).

Combinative Change. Sound change dependent on phonetic surroundings: historical *r* disappears in Southern English before a consonant or pause.

Compound. Word formed by joining two or more others, as 'blackbird', 'lighthousekeeper'.

Conjugation. The list or listing of the inflexions of a verb, as 'love, loves, loved, loved', 'sing, sings, sang, sung'; the classification of verbs according to such inflexions, as 'love' weak, 'sing' strong.

Consonant. Speech sound articulated by partial or complete obstruction of the oral chamber; a letter standing for such a sound, as English 's', 'b'.

Conversion. Creation of a new word from an old one a different part of speech, as verb and noun from conjunction in 'But me no buts!'

Declension. The list or listing of the inflexions of a noun or pronoun, as 'man, man's, men, men's', 'he, him, his'; the classification of nouns according to such inflexions, as 'boy' regular, 'man' irregular.

Dental. Speech sound articulated with the tongue touching the backs of the upper front teeth, as—sometimes—initial and final in 'dent', 'tend'.

Derivation. Formation of a word by addition of an affix to another word, as 'warmth' from 'warm', 'reproduce' from 'produce', 'manly' and 'manliness' from 'man' and 'manly' (but 'man's' from 'man' is inflexion).

Diachronic. Said of the historical study of language; see **Synchronic.**

Dialect. Form of a language used by a constituent speech-community of that language, regional (e.g., southern), class (e.g., middle), or occupational (e.g., literary).

Digraph. Combination of two letters to spell one sound, as initial and final in 'thrash'.

Diphthong. Vowel in one syllable, but with movement of the speech organs from one position to another during the course of articulation, as in 'high', 'how'.

Doublet. Word differing (in form, meaning, or both) from another from a common source, as 'chief', 'chef'; 'paternal', 'fatherly'.

Etymology. Derivation and history of a word's form and meaning; the study thereof.

Folk Etymology. Alteration in popular use of an unfamiliar word to a more familiar form, as 'crayfish' from French *crevisse*, 'crab' (unrelated to 'fish').

Fricative. Consonant articulated by partial obstruction (and consequent friction) in the oral chamber; the initial and final sounds in 'vice', 'fish', 'those'.

Gender. Categories of nouns and pronouns in modern English, revealed in form ('governor', 'governess') or more often reference ('the boy ... he', 'the girl ... she', 'the house ... it'). Gender may be natural ('boy', 'girl') or grammatical ('the ship ... she').

Generalization. Broadening of the semantic content of a word, as modern 'quarantine', 'isolation of any duration', originally one of forty days.

Glide. Speech sounds made during movement of speech organs, therefore heard in diphthongs and semi-vowels; also in 'milk', 'bite'.

Glottis. Opening between the vocal cords; its closure produces a *glottal stop*, as in some pronunciations of 'out', 'bottle'.

Gradation. Systematic variation of the root vowel in conjugation, as 'sing, sang, sung'.

Grammar. The formal systems of linguistic patterning, including phonology, morphology, and syntax; the study thereof.

Homophone. Word which duplicates in sound another which it differs from in origin, meaning, and often spelling, as 'knight : night'.

Ideogram. Symbol standing for a meaning, like '5', rather than for a word, like 'five'. Some languages use or used wholly ideogrammatic writing.

Idiolect. Form of language used by a single member of a speech community, standing in much the same relation to dialect as dialect to language.

Idiom. Construction whose meaning is not merely the sum of the meanings of its constituents, but has to be learned separately, as 'ice cream'. Thus all morphemes are idioms, but only some words and a few phrases.

Infix. Affix inserted within a word.

Inflexion. Grammatical variation of a word by affix through declension ('man, man's, men, men's'; 'he, him, his'), conjugation ('love, loves, loved, loved'), or comparison ('long, longer, longest'); usually by suffix following any derivational suffix ('childhood's', 'beautifies').

Interdental. Fricative articulated with the tongue between the teeth; the initial sounds in 'thy', 'thigh'.

Intonation. The pattern of pitch in spoken language.

Isogloss. Line on a map showing the geographical boundary between two linguistic features, or the limit of one.

Isolative. Syntactical system depending on invariable (usually monosyllabic) roots, and therefore on word order; basis of Chinese.

Isolative Change. Sound change independent of phonetic surroundings: all Chaucer's 'ee' sounds are now 'ai'.

Labial. Consonant articulated with the lips; the initial and final sounds in 'pub', 'warm'.

Labiodental. Consonant articulated with the lower lip and upper front teeth; the initial and final sounds in 'five'.

Language. The human capacity for communication by significant systems of spoken sound; any one such system, composed of all its mutually intelligible dialects.

Lateral. Consonant articulated by blocking the centre of the mouth with the tongue, at the sides of which the air passes; the initial and final sounds in 'lull'.

Lax. Speech sound articulated with relatively little tenseness of tongue and jaw; all the sounds in 'bid'.

Lexis. The free items patterned by formal systems of grammar in a language; vocabulary; the study thereof.

Liquid. Consonant articulated without obstruction or friction, somewhat like a vowel; the initial and final sounds in 'rule'.

Loan Word. Word borrowed and naturalized from one language into another, as English 'garage' (from French), 'dungaree' (Hindustani).

Long Vowel. One of the monophthongs classed together by their common history, similar duration and tendency to develop a slight glide, as in 'beat', 'bait', 'boot', 'boat', 'bought', 'bard', 'Bert'.

Monophthong. Vowel in one syllable articulated without movement of the speech organs and hence constant in sound quality throughout its duration, as in 'bit', 'boot'.

Mood. Categories of conjugation indicating some aspect of the speaker's attitude toward the action, as 'He goes' (indicative), 'If he go' (subjunctive), 'Go' (imperative).

Morpheme. Minimum meaningful formal unit in any language, discussed on pp. 61–2.

Morphology. The arrangement of morphemes in words; the study thereof.

Mutation. Modification of a vowel by the influence of another (sometimes vanished) in the next syllable, resulting in pairs like 'mouse, mice', 'man, men'.

Nasal. Consonant articulated with the nasal passage open; the initial, medial and final sounds in 'meaning'.

Number. Category of inflexion, signalled by declension ('boy, boys'; 'I, we'), conjugation ('goes, go') and agreement among several parts of speech ('This boy goes; These boys go'). Now the contrast is between singular and plural, but in early English between singular, dual and plural.

Onomatopoeia. Echoism, the formation of words by imitation of a natural sound, as 'buzz', 'crunch'.

Open Syllable. One ending with a vowel, as both in 'auto'.

Open Vowel. One articulated with the tongue low in the mouth; the vowel sounds in 'hot', 'hope'.

Orthography. System of representing language in writing; the study of such.

Palatal. Consonant articulated with the tongue near the hard part (palate) of the roof of the mouth; the initial and final sounds in 'yoke', 'hog'.

Paradigm. A set of forms representing the inflexion of a word or of a part of speech.

Parts of Speech. Categories into one or more of which all items in the lexis of a language may fit according to their inflexional characteristics and positional availability.

Pejoration. Degradation of the semantic content of a word, as modern 'lust', originally simply 'pleasure'.

Person. Category of declension ('I, you, he; we, you, they') and conjugation ('Am, are, is; are, are') distinguishing between speaker (first p.), spoken to (second p.) and spoken of (third p.).

Phoneme. Minimum significant sound unit in any language, discussed on pp. 60–1.

Phonetics. The analysis, description and classification of the production and characteristics of speech sounds.

Phonology. The sound system of language, regarded either diachronically or sychronically; the study thereof.

Phrase. A free grammatical unit of two or more words without a finite verb.

Pitch. Tonal height or depth of sound musically, i.e. in vibrations per second; a linguistic feature of contrast, as between 'where' with a rising and with a falling pitch.

Plosive. Stop with abrupt release, as the initial sounds in 'pad', 'dope', 'kid'.

Prefix. Affix added before a word, as 'reproduce' (from 'produce').

Reduplication. Formation of a word by partial repetition of another, as 'helter-skelter', 'fiddle-faddle'.

Root. Irreducible base common to all derived forms, as 'wed' in 'wedding', 'wedder', 'wedded'.

Round Vowel. Vowel in producing which the lips round and protrude, as in 'round' and 'protrude'.

Semantics. Study of the meanings of speech forms, especially lexis, both functionally and historically.

Semi-vowel. Glide beginning a syllable, and so usually represented in spelling, unlike transitional glides; the initial sounds in 'yet', 'wet'.

Sentence. A linguistic structure not a constituent of another one.

Short Vowel. One of the monophthongs classed together by their common history, similar duration and lack of tendency to develop a slight glide, as in 'bit', 'bet', 'foot', 'pot', 'but', 'bat'.

Specialization. Narrowing of the semantic content of a word, as 'starve', 'die through hunger', originally simply 'die'.

Spelling Pronunciation. Pronunciation unduly influenced by unphonetic spelling, e.g., by the 'l' in 'walk'; see p. 40.

Spirant. Same as **Fricative**.

Stem. Root plus any derivational (but no inflexional) affix, as 'kind', 'kindly', 'kindliness'.

Stop. Consonant articulated by complete obstruction of the oral chamber; the initial and final sounds in 'dog', 'pick', 'bit'.

Stress. Relative prominence of a syllable in loudness. There are three levels of stress in '*TELephone*'.

Strong Verb. One in which the conjugation is chiefly by gradation rather than by suffix, as 'sing, sang, sung'.

Suffix. Affix added at the end of a word, as 'producer' and 'produces' —derivation and inflexion (from 'produce').

Syllabic. Forming a syllable, especially final consonant sounds as in 'button', 'bottle', 'chasm'.

Syllable. Sound unit within an utterance having a separate peak of loudness, usually on a vowel.

Synchronic. Said of the study of a language at a single point in time; see **Diachronic**.

Syntax. The arrangement of words in phrases, clauses and sentences; the study thereof.

Synthetic. Syntactical system depending on declension, differentiating between *Johannes Mariam amat* and *Johannem Maria amat*; basis of Latin (and Old English).

Tense. 1. Speech sound articulated with relatively little laxness of tongue and jaw, as all the sounds in 'fight'.

2. Category of conjugation distinguishing between present and past ('love, loved'). Further distinctions made by the use of verbs like 'might', 'will', are phrases, not tenses.

Umlaut. Same as **Mutation.**

Velar. Consonant articulated with the tongue near the soft part (velum) of the roof of the mouth; the initial and final sounds in 'king' and 'wig'.

Voice. 1. The buzzing of the vocal chords discussed on p. 60. All vowels have 'voice'. So have the initial and final sounds in 'dog', 'those', but not in 'tack', 'thatch'.

2. Categories of verb phrases contrasting 'active' and 'passive'. A clause is in the passive voice if it contains part of the verb 'be' and the past participle of a transitive verb, and can be transformed into an active clause.

Vowel. A voiced speech sound produced without obstruction of the oral chamber; a letter standing for such a sound.

Weak Declension. Classes of nouns and adjectives in Germanic languages (including Old English) with declensional suffixes chiefly in *-n*. Weak nouns are such by their nature; weak adjectives, by position.

Weak Verbs. One in which the conjugation is chiefly by suffix rather than by gradation, as 'love, loved, loved'.

Word. Minimum unit of form and meaning capable of standing alone. Some, but not all, morphemes (and a few phonemes) are words at the same time. A form with two or more units capable of standing alone is a compound.

Index